Project Planning,
Scheduling
& Control

Project Planning, Scheduling & Control

A Hands-On Guide to
Bringing Projects In On Time and On Budget

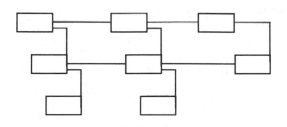

James P. Lewis

PROBUS PUBLISHING COMPANY
Chicago, Illinois
Cambridge, England

This publication is designed to provide accurate and authoritative information in regard to the subject matter covered. It is sold with the
understanding that the publisher is not engaged in rendering legal,
accounting, or other professional service.

Authorization to photocopy items for internal or personal use, or the
internal or personal use of specific clients, is granted by PROBUS
PUBLISHING COMPANY, provided that the U.S. $7.00 per page fee
is paid directly to Copyright Clearance Center, 27 Congress Street,
Salem, MA 01970, USA; Phone: 1-508-744-3350. For those organizations that have been granted a photocopy license by CCC, a separate
system of payment has been arranged. The fee code for users of the
Transactional Reporting Service is 1-55738-204-2/91/$00.00 + $7.00.

Illustrations by Lea Ann Lewis.

Library of Congress Catalogue Card Number: 91-60939

CIP Data Applied For

ISBN 1-55738-204-2

Printed in the United States of America

BC

4   5   6   7   8   9   0

To my father
Moffet Palmer Lewis,
his wife, Alice,
my mother,
Hazel Inez McDaniel,
and my sister
Priscilla Ann Atwell

Contents

List of Figures

List of Tables

Preface

Nearly twenty-five years ago, as a young electrical engineer, I managed my first project. The company I worked for hoped to sell communications equipment to the Brazilian government, and I was to prepare sample units to send to Sao Paulo for evaluation. Of course, the units had to be flawless, and this demand placed a lot of pressure on us. There were hundreds of details to cover, and the people assigned to do the work did not normally report to me—so my first project was organized as a matrix.

I would like to say that I really *managed* the project, but that would not be truthful. I actually performed more the role of *gopher* than project manager, and even though the job was successfully completed, it was not to my credit; I simply had good people working on it.

Like most newly appointed project managers, I had no training in project management. I didn't know the difference between a CPM diagram and an airline schedule, and it was several years before that changed. At the time, I didn't even have a book on project management, which is one reason why I have written this one.

This book is for the new, or relatively inexperienced project manager, who may be asking, as I did, "Where do I start, and what do I do next?" It is written for the *practicing* project manager, regardless of his or her discipline. (It should also be helpful to experienced project managers in two ways—in offering help to new managers, and to remind themselves of the "basics," which we sometimes forget.)

It is fashionable today to write books on managing projects in terms of specific disciplines. Following that practice, we have Data Processing Project Management, Construction Project Management, Engineering Project Management, and so on. There is nothing wrong with this approach.

However, the implication is that the method varies as the discipline changes, and I don't agree with that suggestion. Of course, there are some fundamental differences, but just as addition, subtraction, multiplication, and division are used in virtually every walk of life, there are also certain basic tools which are common to project management in *all* areas of work, whether it be engineering, construction, banking, data processing, marketing, or software development. I have tried to write this book so that it will be useful to the project manager in *any* discipline or environment.

The major focus of this book is the presentation of the essential *tools and techniques* of project management—how to plan, schedule, and control, using the *Work Breakdown Structure* (WBS), *Critical Path Method* (CPM) or PERT scheduling, and Earned Value Analysis. There are no case studies, but there are real-world anecdotes and some pseudo-fictional examples, which I have used in an effort to make the subject a *living* topic, rather than simply a boring, academic dissertation. Case studies are fine, once you have a firm understanding of the tools. Without such knowledge, the case study loses its impact.

The book also contains no specialized or advanced material, such as methods of contract administration, bid preparation, multicultural project management, or military project reporting, because most new project managers would not be handling such areas (and God help them if they are). There are a number of good books available which deal with those topics, and the reader will find some of them cited in the reading list at the end of this book.

However, even though this is an introductory book, it is not a fill-in-the blank kind of "cookbook," to be used as a crutch. Such rote behavior is not managing, but robotics. There are some forms, a checklist, and a sample project plan included, which I hope will be useful in managing your own projects, but I have tried to explain the *whys* and *wherefores* so that you do not blindly proceed, with great haste, on your way to disaster.

I have also added considerable emphasis on the use of the personal computer in project scheduling, with particular attention to the problem of allocating resources. One of the major causes of project failure is the inability to deal effectively with resource allocation. Chapter Seven is devoted entirely to this subject, using *Project Workbench*™ as an example of what can be done by applying state-of-the art software.

Finally, I think it is important to stress that project management is really "people management," and I have presented ways of dealing with the "people" issues which must be addressed in order to make the tools work. Very early in my career, I found that I solved technical problems with ease—if only I could resolve my "people" problems.

It is customary to thank everyone who has contributed to the creation of a book, and I would like to do that. Unfortunately, if I were to list all of those who have contributed to this book, that would be a book in itself. For nearly ten years I have been teaching project management seminars throughout the United States, Puerto Rico, and Canada, and I seldom teach a class in which I do not learn something from a participant. So, to all of the many students who have challenged me to think and who have shared their experiences with me, I owe a special debt and a lot of gratitude.

One individual does merit special mention. I have had many long discussions with an eminent practitioner of project management, Mr. Norman Smith, of the Torrington Company, and he has generously shared with me the fruits of his many years of experience, much of which has contributed greatly to this book. A special thanks goes to him.

Finally, my wife, Lea Ann, has spent countless hours reading the text and creating illustrations which, had I done them, would have yielded stale renditions with no "spark" at all. She has created illustrations that not only have vitality but also support the educational character of this book. She has encouraged me to make this book the best it can possibly be. Much of what is good about the book, I owe to her. The weaknesses are, of course, my own.

Jim Lewis
Vinton, Virginia

Section One

Introduction to Project Management

CHAPTER 1 # Introduction to Project Management

In 2650 B.C. Imhotep built the step pyramid for the pharaoh Zoser at Sakkare, in Egypt. About 150 years later and 2200 miles away, the ancestors of the British began building stone henges and circles throughout the British Isles. The best known of these is Stonehenge.

Another 500 years passed, and the Mayans had become a recognizable political group in Central America, who peppered the barren landscape of the Yucatan Peninsula with magnificent temples at such sites as Chichen Itza, Sayil, and Uxmal.

The builders of these remarkable structures were the world's first project managers. They had no computers to assist them, no PERT (Performance Evaluation and Review Techniques) or CPM (Critical Path Method) scheduling tools, and in some cases not even paper on which to

draw plans. Yet they managed some exceptionally complex projects, using the simplest of tools.

Managing projects dates back at least 4500 years, yet the role of project manager is only recently becoming recognized as a discipline in its own right. Some universities are beginning to offer courses in project management, and at least one university is offering a Master of Business Administration degree with a concentration in project management. In addition, with the advent of scheduling software that runs on personal computers, interest in project management is growing at a rapid rate.

What Is a Project?

There are all kinds of projects. There are projects to develop new products, to develop a marketing plan, to build a large office building, to remodel a home, to landscape one's lawn, to develop a new vaccine and so on. The possibilities are almost endless, making project management a nearly universal discipline. One commonly accepted definition of a project is as follows:

> A project is a one-time job that has defined start-ing and ending dates, a clearly specified objective, or scope of work to be performed, a predefined budget, and usually a temporary or-ganization that is dismantled once the project is completed.

The key words here are *one-time, schedule* (starting and ending dates), *budget*, and *objectives/scope.* Through these, a project is differentiated from repetitive activities such as production and order processing.

Even for such seemingly repetitive activities as building homes using the same designs over and over, there are variables that will make each construction job unique: the terrain will be different, the weather will vary, or the work group will change. It is the uniqueness of each project that makes special demands on project managers and simultaneously makes project manage-ment an exciting discipline.

What Is Project Management?

First, it might be good to say what project management *is not.* It is not just scheduling. With the growth in popu-larity of personal-computer-based scheduling software, many people think that if they simply buy the software and apply it, they will be doing sound project manage-ment. Then they find that they really do not know how to apply the software.

As a matter of fact, this is putting the "cart before the horse," since it is very difficult to know what soft-ware to buy unless you first have a good grasp of how to manage projects and exactly what you are going to do with the software.

For example, do you need to do multiple-project re-source allocation? If so, you probably need one of the more powerful packages. If you are running a few small projects, on the other hand, you can use one of the less powerful (and less expensive) programs. But this is get-ting ahead of ourselves. Let us return to what project management actually *is.*

Figure 1.1

Good, Fast, Cheap

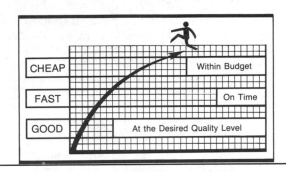

For many years it has been customary to say that project management is the planning, scheduling, and controlling of project activities to achieve *performance, dollar,* and *time* objectives, for a given scope of work. These have been referred to as PDT objectives. Recently, a participant in a project management seminar which I taught said that he calls the objectives *good, fast,* and *cheap.* These more colorful terms certainly capture the essence of what a project manager must achieve, as shown in Figure 1.1.

It is important to note that the three objectives must be met *while using resources efficiently and effectively.* This is a key point in project management, and one which is too often overlooked. In every organization, resources are limited, and unless the project manager can deal successfully with the resource allocation problem, he or she will not be successful. Experience shows that in many environments failure to properly manage resources is one of the most common causes of project failure. Methods of allocating resources will be covered in more detail in the scheduling section of the book.

As for the *good, fast, and cheap* objectives (GFC), the important thing to note is that they cannot all be tied down simultaneously. If two are specified, the third must be allowed to vary. This is illustrated in Figure 1.2. This assumes, of course, that the scope of the project remains constant. If scope varies, then the other variables will change as well.

In contrast with project management, general management is concerned with more repetitive tasks, such

Figure 1.2

Good, Fast, Cheap:
Pick Two

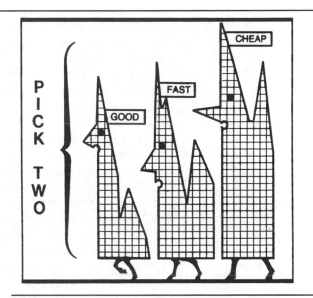

as manufacturing processes, and generally involves the use of the same group of people on a continuing basis. The general manager usually runs a department, which is typically hierarchical in nature, with clearly defined authority over subordinates. In contrast, a project manager often manages a team over which he or she has no real authority. To compensate for this lack of authority, a project manager must develop effective interpersonal skills, especially in terms of interpersonal influence.

The Project Team

A team is a group of individuals who collectively work to meet a common objective to which they are all committed. Unless commitment to project objectives is obtained from all members of the team, the project is very unlikely to be successful.

Therefore, project managers must work hard to develop commitment of team members to the project itself. In fact, building a project team is crucial to success, and teambuilding is not a once-and-forever event which consists of bringing the group together and saying to them, "Okay, troops, your objective is to do thus and so. Now you're a team. Get to it!"

We can learn a lot from sports teams in this regard. No sports team could be successful without *practice, practice, practice.* However, there is more to success than practice. They must be sure they are correcting their performance deficits, or else they might *get really good at playing poorly!* The same is true of a project team. For this reason, a project manager must know how to turn a group of individuals into a real team.

Unfortunately, while sports teams understand the need to work on improving the *process* by which they do their "work," teams in organizations tend to become so focused on the *task* to be done that they lose sight of this need. So, while it is outside the scope of this book to cover teambuilding, every project manager must work hard on building his or her team by paying attention to process issues—that is, the way in which people work together, not just the task itself. Process issues include communication, conflict, leadership styles, hidden agendas and so on. Teambuilding is the effort invested in dealing with these factors so that they do not keep the project team from achieving its objectives.

The Nature of Projects

While the nature of projects will vary somewhat with the content of the work being done, there are a number of similarities independent of content. When effort by many disciplines within an organization is required, the project is called *multi-disciplinary.* The use of a number of disciplines creates special problems in that everyone does not speak a "common language." Each discipline has its own jargon, its own technical difficulties and its own "tools of the trade," thus making communication and understanding difficult to achieve.

Most projects have a life cycle which consists of six phases—*Concept, Definition, and Planning, Design, Development or Construction, Application, and Post-Completion.* Whether all six phases are involved is determined by the exact nature of the work, but certainly every project can be thought of as going through some stages. The following points always apply:

- The character of the program changes in each life-cycle phase (see Figure 1.5).
- The uncertainty regarding the ultimate time and cost diminishes as each phase is completed.

Unfortunately, too many projects go through a life cycle that looks like the one illustrated in Figure 1.3. One of the primary causes of this failure is a ready-fire-aim approach, in which the push is to "get on with it," with too little attention being paid to just what it is that should be done.

Project management is really problem-solving on a large scale, and the first step in all problem-solving is to make sure the problem is defined correctly. Otherwise, one is likely to develop the *right solution* to the *wrong problem!*

One current approach to improving quality is called *Total Quality Management,* and emphasizes that we can achieve any one of the four results shown in Figure 1.4.

Naturally, we want to do "right things right," but failure to properly define the problem will lead to one of the other three results. As can be concluded from examining Figure 1.3, definition of requirements came after the project turned into a nightmare, and this failure to define requirements at the beginning is exactly what caused the nightmare in the first place. Figure 1.5 illustrates the life-cycles as they should be in the typical project.

The Life-Cycle Phases

Concept Phase

The *concept phase* of a project is the point at which someone identifies a need that must be met. It can be for a new product or service, a move from one location to another, a new banking service, an advertising campaign, or a research program. At the concept phase, there is only a fuzzy definition of the problem to be solved. In fact, note that a *feasibility study* may have to be conducted in order to clarify the definition of the project before proceeding to the next phase.

Definition and Planning Phase

In fact, it is the *definition and planning phase* of the project that is intended to tie down exactly what is to be

Figure 1.3

Incorrect Life-Cycle

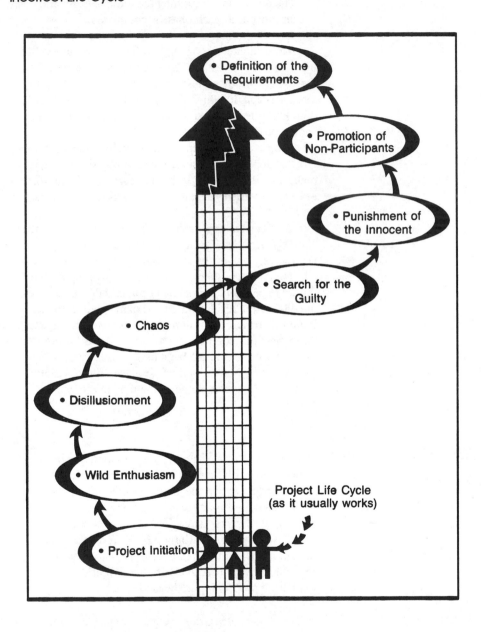

Figure 1.4

Total Quality
Management

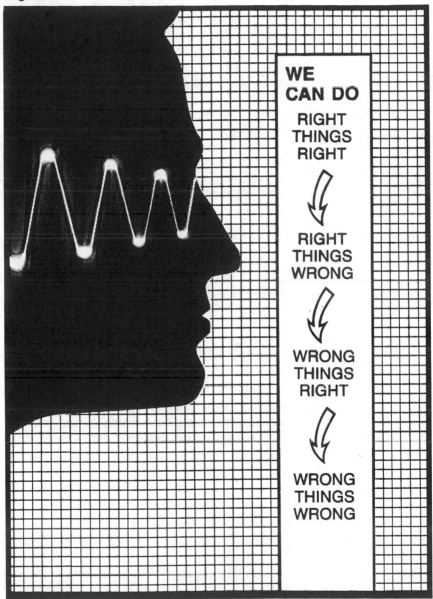

done. A problem statement is developed, which is meant to define the problem to be solved very concretely. This is, of course, the ideal way of doing it. There are some projects in which the project definition will continue to evolve as work progresses, simply because neither the "customer" nor the project team is able to fully define what the customer needs.

In any case, once a suitable definition has been written, objectives are developed, strategies for achieving them are selected, and detailed working plans are constructed to ensure that those objectives are achieved.

During this stage, an organization is established by identifying those individuals who will participate in the project, deciding to whom they will report and defining the limits of their authority, responsibility, and accountability. Note also that a control system is developed, quality assurance procedures are set up (if they do not already exist) and detailed planning is completed.

When the plan is finished, it is placed in a *project notebook*, which then serves as the controlling document throughout the life of the project. The notebook is a very useful organizing device for project management, and may actually be a number of ring binders for very large projects.

Design Phase

The *design phase* may not exist (as in a construction project) or may be combined with the development phase. If it does exist, note that there is provision for revising cost and performance targets. Although this idea is "heretical" to some managers, like it or not, one often finds during design of new products or services that original cost, schedule or performance targets cannot be met.

Winston Churchhill once remarked that we must have the right to be smarter today than we were yesterday. Because no one can forecast with 20/20 vision, changes to original targets must be made as new information becomes available.

As of this writing, there is controversy in Congress about the fate of the B-1 bomber, and one congressman recently declared that he wanted it to "cost what they say it will cost." Yet this program has spanned a decade,

Figure 1.5

Project Life-Cycle

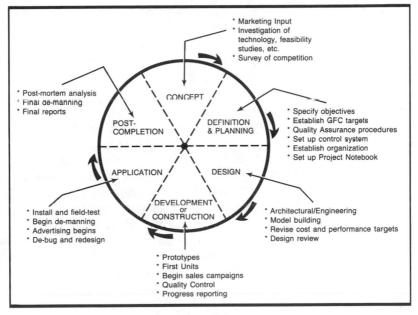

and it is doubtful that anyone, including this outraged congressman, could accurately forecast the cost of such a complex project over such an extended time frame.

Development or Construction Phase

The *development* or *construction phase* is the point at which completed products and services can be tested to see if they meet all performance targets. In the case of new product development, sales campaigns usually begin here. The danger, of course, is that if any serious glitches are discovered in the product after the sales campaign is launched, the organization may be placed in the very difficult (if not disastrous) position of not being able to meet promised deliveries.

Application Phase

Application of the product or service can also yield some unhappy results if problems are discovered; therefore, it is important that products be field tested before being shipped to customers. Software development companies usually ask some of their customers to beta-test their products, so that glitches can be uncovered and corrected before any advertising campaign is begun to the general public.

Horror stories abound, however, of some major companies that have fallen into the trap of shipping products before thorough testing was completed, only to incur considerable expenses repairing or replacing defective products later.

Post-Completion Phase

The *post-completion phase* sounds contradictory at first glance. If the project is complete, how can this be a phase? This phase is, in fact, *aborted* in many projects. Note that it involves a *post-mortem* analysis of the project. For future reference, the project manager should look back at the project and ask what was done well and what was not. If the post-mortem is not done, it is likely that the mistakes of yesterday will be repeated.

One suggestion about post-mortems: they should be done at each major milestone in the project, so that you can take advantage of what you learn for the current project as well as for future ones.

The Project Management System

In order to manage projects successfully, certain key elements must be in place in the organization. In systems terminology, these elements together constitute a project management system, and each individual element is a subsystem. Because all systems consist of *inputs, outputs,* and some *process* for transforming those inputs into outputs, the same can be said for each component of a project management system.

The project management system consists of seven components, or subsystems, as shown in the diagram in Figure 1.6.

Planning System

Of the seven components shown, the *planning system* is perhaps the most important, since, if a poor plan is developed, it may be impossible to execute the project successfully. As was stated previously, there is often a tendency to adopt a *ready-fire-aim* approach, which is to just do something, regardless of whether it is right or not.

14

Figure 1.6

Project Management
System

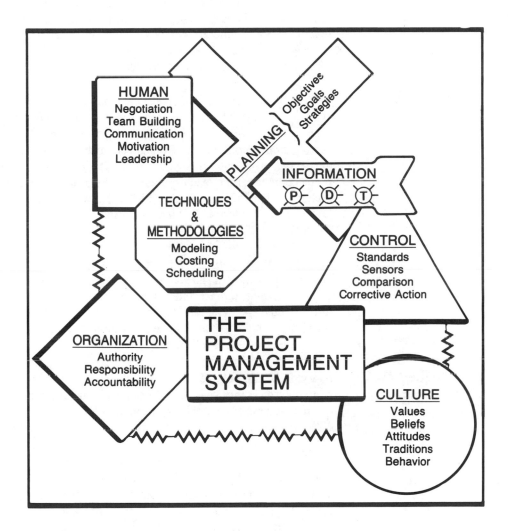

People are often so task-oriented that there seems to be a belief that everyone must be doing something task-related or they are wasting time. Planning is seen as not producing results, and so is considered a waste of time. It is almost as if the manager were saying, "I don't have time to plan—I have work to do!" In the planning section of the book, concrete evidence will be presented to show why such an attitude is unacceptable, and why it leads to problems in managing projects.

Information System

The *information system* gathers the data that must be available so a project manager knows whether a project is on target. However, that information must be *timely,* and one of the problems some organizations have is that the data on project status is gathered, fed into a mainframe computer, then batch-processed and distributed at such large time intervals as to make the information useless in terms of control. This issue is further discussed in the control section of the book.

Control System

Control of a project is one of the major responsibilities of a project manager. The control system must use data on project status to determine where the project is with respect to the plan, and initiate corrective action if there is a significant discrepancy. Note that a monitoring system alone is not a control system.

Techniques & Methodologies System

Every project makes use of certain *techniques and methodologies* to get the work done. These might include certain technology, computer-aided design, PERT and CPM scheduling, and costing models.

Organization System

In order to coordinate the efforts of people, an *organization* is established, which must define the limits of authority, responsibility, and accountability of participants. In the section on control, this issue will be discussed in depth, but here it is worth pointing out that if members of the project team have *no* authority, then they will feel no responsibility for their actions and the project manager will have to make all decisions. As William Oncken has written, the result is that the project manager will find himself or herself with monkeys on his back all the time.[1]

Culture System

The *culture* of an organization is the combined effect of the values, beliefs, attitudes, traditions, and behaviors of the members of that entity. The culture of the organization is essentially defined when someone says, "We don't do it that way around here." To violate the cultural expectations of powerful members of an organization is to invite trouble.

If an organization has been practicing "seat-of-the-pants" project management, adopting a formal, disciplined system requires a change in the culture of that organization. The major change is that projects must be properly *planned,* and the initial response will often be that it takes too much time and ties up too many resources.

In addition, in market-driven organizations, the sales staff can no longer make delivery commitments to customers without first consulting the development group. This, too, will raise objections. Sales people may argue that they need to meet the customer's delivery requirements in order to make sales. There is certainly no argument with such a statement.

However, my experience with organizations that operate this way is that such deadlines are often not met simply because they were unrealistic to begin with or they are met through the application of premium labor (overtime rates). Further, customers often have more flexibility on their required dates than sales people want to admit. Suffice it to say that successful project management requires *cooperation* among all the groups involved and provides the tools whereby *realistic* delivery dates can be determined in advance of commitments to customers.

It is also worth noting that the introduction of formal project management is often resisted because people see nothing in it for themselves. In fact, all they see are the "costs" involved. To gain acceptance of the discipline, members of the organization must see that there is some benefit to themselves, rather than a penalty. Unfortunately, it is the time required to plan a project which is seen as a penalty. It takes time and experience to see that the planning done up-front translates into fewer headaches later on.

Human System

Perhaps the most difficult aspect of managing projects is the *human* part. As a comedian said once, "The world would be a pretty good place to live in if it weren't for people." In fact, *none of the tools of project management are of any value if you can't get people to use them.*

Figure 1.7

Skills Required by
Management Level

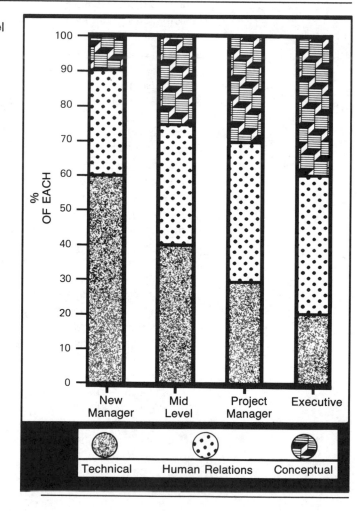

For this reason, project managers need very good interpersonal, or human relations skills. These include the ability to provide proper leadership for team members; the ability to negotiate with customers, team members and other managers for needed resources; skills in building a team; good communication skills; and a knowledge of how to motivate team members when necessary. Figure 1.7 shows how a person's skills must change as he or she moves from being an entry-level manager to a higher-level manager.

As shown in Figure 1.7, a manager needs fewer technical skills, greater conceptual skills (the ability to see the "big picture") and good human relations skills as he or she advances in the organization. The section on the project manager's role discusses this in more detail.

Key Points

- A project is a one-time job, rather than a repetitive process.

- Good, fast, cheap—pick two.

- A project team must be built over time.

- Failure to define a project correctly may lead to failure.

- A post-mortem should be conducted at each major milestone in the project, with a final one being done once the project is completed.

- A project manager needs good human relations skills to get the job done.

Section Two

Project Planning

CHAPTER 2 A General Approach to Planning

Suppose the CEO of a company in Raleigh, North Carolina called in one of her people and said, "We have a real emergency situation in Shelbyville, Tennessee. I want you to get out there right away and fix it. You know, of course, that you'll have to drive the service van, because it has all the equipment that you'll need to work on the problem."

"Got it. I'll get going right away," says the service person.

With that, he rushes out of the CEO's office, back to his desk, starts frantically packing his briefcase and running around like a chicken with its head cut off.

"What's happening?" one of his co-workers asks.

"Got to get to Shelbyville in a hurry," says the service person.

"Have you been there before?"

"No, never."

"How are you going to go—Interstate 40?"

"Don't know."

"Don't you have a map?"

"Nope. Don't have time to worry about a map just now. Just have to get there."

Clearly, this person is headed for trouble. If he really has to get to Shelbyville in the fastest time, he definitely needs a map since he has never been there before.

You might say, "He really is stupid. No one would do that." Yet there are project managers who run projects in the same way all of the time. They have no plan (map) and will tell you they don't have time to make one. Is it any wonder they wind up lost out in the boonies? (Figuratively speaking, of course.)

Everyone knows that one of the key functions that managers perform is planning. Yet experience also shows that many managers either do very little or no planning, or that the plans they do put together are sadly inadequate.

As widely evidenced, the results are often disastrous.[1] Nevertheless, managers don't seem to learn the lessons taught by countless case studies.

> "Plans are worthless, but planning is everything."
> President Dwight D. Eisenhower,
> November 17, 1957

Working without a plan is, of course, the ready-fire-aim approach mentioned in Chapter One. What is not understood by many managers is that they are not in control when they use this approach, even though they will readily agree that being in control is one of the primary requirements of a manager.

Perhaps they have lost sight of what is meant by management control. Control consists of comparing where you are with where you are supposed to be, then taking action to correct for any deviation from target.

Since the way you know where you are supposed to be is by reference to a plan, then without a plan, there is nothing to track progress against.

> Therefore if you have no plan, control is impossible!

One of the most frequent reasons for not planning is summed up by the statement, "I don't have time to plan." When people tell me this, my response is, "Then you spend a lot of time in crisis management."

"Is there any other way?" they ask, verifying that firefighting is a way-of-life for many of them.

The problem is, crisis management is a vicious circle: you don't have time to plan because you are too busy putting out fires, but you have to put out a lot of fires because you have no plan...and around and around you go.

There is only one way out—and it is to simply "bite the bullet" and start developing plans. You will probably fail to achieve them more often than not at first, but over time, if you stick with it, your efforts will pay off.

The motto of the manager who consistently works without a plan might be stated this way:

> We don't know where we're going, but we're getting there awfully fast.

Mistakes in Planning

Even when managers plan, there are at least two common mistakes made. One is to not involve the people who must implement the plan in the planning process. This is either done by the manager who plans unilaterally or by the organization that makes use of a planning group. Either way, there is likely to be difficulty with implementation because of inaccurate estimates, over-looked work or lack of commitment on the part of the people who must execute the plan.

A manager who plans other people's work without soliciting any input from them is likely to expect them to do the work in less time than is possible. This seems to be a common error, probably caused by the fact that the manager is using a self-based estimate. It may very well be that the manager could do the job in the estimated time, but that will not necessarily be true for the individual assigned to do it.

Further, managers often fail to consider that the person for whom they are planning is not working full-time on the project activity, so that the total elapsed time required to do the job is considerably greater than the time allowed.

The net result of giving someone a plan for which they had no input is that they will often react by saying, "There's no way I can do it that fast." With that reaction, the plan is doomed to failure at the outset.

The Project Notebook

In Chapter One, I said that a project notebook is an excellent device for documenting and controlling a project. Ideally, a complete written project plan should be prepared prior to the time work is started. Realistically, the work may be started before the plan is complete, but the plan should still be put together as quickly as possible, before the work has progressed very far.

The plan should define the objectives of the project, the approach to be taken and the commitments being assumed by the manager and key contributors.

The plan should cover the general topics listed below. This list can, in fact, be considered a table of contents for the project plan. It should be housed in a notebook (or notebooks, for large projects), and copies should be distributed to key members of the project team.

Problem Statement

This is a definition of the problem to be solved by the project. As stated in an earlier section of this book, without a sound definition of the problem, one is likely to waste valuable resources by developing the right solution to the wrong problem. Techniques for defining problems follow in this chapter.

Project Mission Statement

This is a summary of the overall goal and purpose of the project, identifying the client and outlining the general approach to be followed in doing the work. A more specific detail of the approach to be followed is also contained in the plan (see the following paragraphs), and details on how to develop a mission statement are presented in Chapter Three.

Program Scope

This is a statement of what *will* and *will not* be done in the project. It establishes boundaries, so that the customer knows what he or she will get when the project is completed. See comments on controlling for *scope creep* later in this chapter.

Objectives

The objectives include technical, profit, performance, quality, and other. There are forms in Chapter Three to be used in writing objectives and conducting a SWOT analysis.

Approach To Be Followed

The mission statement provides only the most cursory statement of the approach to project work. A more specific statement is needed so that other people in the organization can decide if the proposed approach fits in with the strategies preferred by management. For example, are we only going to manage subcontractors? What technical methods will be employed? Is a make-or-buy situation involved?

Contractual Requirements

List all deliverable items—including reports, prototypes, documentation. In projects which require significant reporting (such as military projects), failure to account for the cost to prepare such documentation can result in a cost penalty to the project.

End Item Specifications To Be Met

These would include engineering specifications, software functional specifications, building codes, government regulations, and marketing performance specifications, which position a product against its competition.

Where regulations and other specifications exist in published form, it may be satisfactory to simply cite these. However, internal specs should always be included in the notebook.

Work Breakdown Structure

This is the heart of the plan and serves to tie everything together. It provides a way of estimating resource requirements, total project budget and work scheduling. It also provides an excellent visual display of total project scope. Finally, it can be used as a point-of-reference against which to track progress. Development of work breakdown structures is covered in Chapter Four.

Target Schedules

The plan must include major milestones and detailed task schedules to be used by the people doing the work. Major milestones are dates at which key portions of the project work should be completed; they should involve a *deliverable* whenever possible. By requiring something tangible at a milestone, it is easier to evaluate whether the milestone was actually met as required. Task schedules are the detailed schedules that show how various milestones are going to be achieved.

Required Resources

Resources include people, equipment, facilities and materials. Because every organization has limited resources, success in managing projects depends on the efficient and effective use of those resources. Human resources are best displayed using loading diagrams, which show how many people of a given skill category are being used at any given time. (Or they show how many hours per day a specific individual is to work on the project.) Chapter Seven offers more detail on loading diagrams. These will be used by functional groups to determine if adequate support is available for all projects and, if not, whether to work overtime or seek permanent or temporary staff to provide the required support.

Control System

How will progress be measured and reported? To whom will reports be distributed? How often will measurements be required? If changes are required to the project, how will they be handled and who will pay for them?

Major Contributors

These will usually be group leaders in functional groups. What are the limits of authority, responsibility and accountability of various contributors? One device for showing the level-of-involvement of contributors is the Linear Responsibility Chart, which is presented in Chapter Four.

Risk Areas

In planning a project, it is helpful to ask, "What could go wrong?" By identifying risks, steps can be taken to deal with them proactively rather than reactively. Examples of risks include financial limitations, penalties for non-performance, subcontractor default, work stoppages, technical exposures and other possible problems. See the section in this chapter on conducting a SWOT analysis for more details on how to conduct a risk analysis.

Signoff of the Plan

When the plan is complete, it is submitted to *stakeholders* for approval. Anyone who has a vested interest in the project is a stakeholder. Typical stakeholders include functional managers, managers of project managers, the customer, financial officers of the company, subcontractors and sometimes others.

Customers are always stakeholders. They include both external and internal customers. For example, the marketing department and the manufacturing group can each be considered customers of a product design group.

Each stakeholder signs the plan attesting that as far as his or her area of concern goes, the plan appears to be feasible and appears to properly address those concerns. For example, a functional manager would sign signifying that he or she feels confident that the number of support people required to get the job done will be available when required, and that they will be able to handle the technical requirements of the job.

Once the plan has been approved, it gives the project manager authority to execute and control his or her project to completion. Significant changes in approach or other revisions to the plan that are made after initial approval must be communicated to stakeholders and then approved.

Getting the plan signed off should be done in a meeting. It should not be done by circulating copies of the notebook through company mail and asking people to read and sign it. Under those conditions, they will often fail to read carefully, and when they are later required to "deliver" on their part of the project, they will be unable to do so.

During the sign-off meeting, the project manager should highlight key areas of the project which could be problems and encourage all members of the group to ask "embarrassing" questions about *any* area of the plan. It is better to have those questions asked during the meeting than later.

If possible, the meeting should be held in advance of the start date of the project to allow changes to be made to the plan if necessary. However, as mentioned earlier, the project may be started before the plan can be completed and signed off.

The purpose of getting a plan approved is to ensure that it is realistic and feasible, not to use it as a club to "beat up" on people if there are problems!

Changes to the Plan

The previous section stated that significant changes to the plan should be made and signed off by stakeholders affected by those changes. This may not involve the entire group of stakeholders who signed the plan originally.

What constitutes a significant change must be agreed-upon in advance. For example, a significant change to the budget might be considered to be plus or minus 10 percent. Thus, if during project execution it is determined that total project costs are likely to be 10 percent greater than forecast originally, then new funding would have to be approved by the financial officer, marketing director and engineering director (for example).

Not only should this procedure be followed if the project is forecasted to be overspent, it should also be done if an *underspend* is predicted. I know, this is foolhardy! No one ever gives money back, since they will have their budget cut next time if they do. That is the result of game-playing in organizations, however, and does not constitute proper management practice. Money which is not needed in a project should be freed up as soon as possible so that it can be used elsewhere in the organization. Failure to do so results in what the economists call *opportunity cost* to the organization. The money could have been used in a beneficial way, but the opportunity was lost because funds were already allocated to a project.

One particularly troublesome change is the revision of project scope. Scope defines how much work is going to be done—that is, the *boundaries* of the project. Scope has a way of creeping up during the life of a project. Usually it happens because the client discovers that you can do something he or she didn't know you could do, or finds that the competition has a feature not originally asked for and asks if you can do the additional work.

The trap here is that, in order to be cooperative, the project manager may agree to the added work without asking for additional time, resources or funding. It might in fact be possible to absorb a minor change in scope, because the impact to *good, fast, cheap* is not great. However, when several minor changes are added together, they may collectively result in a significant change, and both the client and the project manager may wind up in trouble.

The client may not want to pay the final bill—but when the client is the marketing department, the bill has already been paid by the company by the time the project is complete, so at that point it is too late to do anything about it.

Furthermore, the project manager often is blamed for coming in over budget. Many at the end of a project may suffer convenient amnesia! No one seems to remember that the scope of the project grew. All they know is that the project manager did not meet original targets.

Watch out for scope creep!

What Is Planning?

Planning is the answering of the following general questions:

- What must be done? This question deals with objectives and magnitude or scope of work.
- How should it be done? Answering this question leads to the selection of project *strategy*.
- Who should do it? Roles and responsibilities can be assigned by answering this question.
- When must it be done? Scheduling is accomplished with this one.
- How much will it cost? The budget is developed.
- How good does it have to be? Quality levels are determined.
- What performance is required? Performance specifications are generated.
- What strengths do we have? How can we best take advantage of them?
- What weaknesses do we have? How do we minimize the impact of those?
- What opportunities does this project present us and how can we capitalize on them?
- What obstacles or threats could keep us from achieving our objectives? Risk analysis.

Note that the last four questions in the list are asked by marketing people and are most easily remembered as a SWOT analysis. (See Figure 2.1.)

Developing a Problem Statement

As mentioned in Chapter One, project management is problem-solving on a large scale. Until a satisfactory definition has been developed, steps to doing the work cannot be devised, since the definition determines the proper approach to take. For example, the question, "What is the best way to put a person on the moon?" is very general and allows many possible strategies to be considered. The question, "How can one build a rocket to put someone on the moon?" however, is more narrowly focused and yields more limited answers.

Figure 2.1

SWOT Analysis

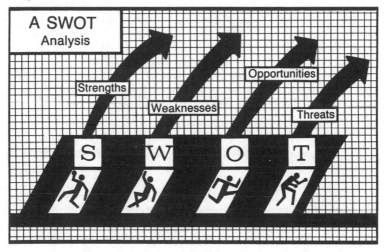

How a problem is defined determines the solution possibilities.

Open- and Close-Ended Problems

An open-ended problem is one that has no single correct answer. It also has boundaries that can be challenged. Because our educational system teaches us to find the one right answer to problems presented, many of us are thereafter unwilling or reluctant to challenge boundaries of real-world problems, even though most such problems are open-ended. Roger von Oech suggests that one way out of this dilemma is to always insist on finding the *second right answer!*

Most projects will involve the solution of open-ended problems. That is, there will be no single approach to apply in solving the problem. However, a few projects might be thought of as fitting into the category of close-ended problems. For example, overhauling a power generator that has developed a fault might be thought of in this way. Once a diagnosis has

The Plan

In the beginning was the plan, and then the specification.

And the plan was without form, and the specification was void.

And darkness was upon the faces of the implementors.

And they spoke unto their manager, saying: *"It is a crock of cow manure, and it stinketh."*

And their manager went to the second level manager, and he spake unto him, saying: *"It is a crock of excrement, and none may abide the odor thereof."*

And the second level manager went to the third level, and he spake unto him saying: *"It is a container of excrement, and it is very strong, such that none may abide before it."*

And the third level went to the division manager, and he spake unto him, saying: *"It is a vessel of fertilizer, and none may abide its strength."*

And the division manager went to the assistant vice-president, and he spake unto him, saying: *"It contains that which aids plant growth, and it is very strong."*

And the assistant vice-president went to the vice-president, and he spake unto him, saying: *"It promoteth growth and it is very powerful."*

And the vice-president went before the president and spake unto him, saying: *"This powerful new product will promote growth of the company."*

And the president looked upon the product and saw that *"It was good!"*

(Source Unknown)

determined the defect in the generator, the approach to repair the unit is fairly well-defined.

However, when there is doubt as to what kind of problem exists, Figure 2.2 should help you determine whether the problem is open- or close-ended. (See page 37.)

Aids in Problem Definition

Once you have determined if the problem is open- or close-ended, you have to develop a formal problem statement (or definition). To help you arrive at a sound problem definition (or redefinition, if you have decided the initial statement is inadequate), refer to Table 2.1.[2]

Phased Planning

It is generally not possible to plan a project of significant duration in detail because, as was stated previously, no project manager has 20/20 foresight. Also, in many

Table 2.1

Problem Definition Aids

1. Write down a general description of the problem under consideration.
2. Now, complete the following statements about the problem. If you cannot think of anything to write for a particular statement, move on to the next one.
   a. There is usually more than one way of looking at problems. You could also define this one as...
   b. ...but the main point of the problem is...
   c. What I would really like to do is...
   d. If I could break all laws of reality (physical, social, etc.) I would try to solve it by...
   e. The problem, put another way, could be likened to...
   f. Another, even stranger, way of looking at it might be...
3. Now return to your original definition (step 1). Write down whether any of the redefinitions have helped you see the problem in a different way.

instances, decisions are made following completion of one phase of project work that impact subsequent work. Attempting to plan a long-term project in great detail only leads to the fruitless attempt to meet a completion date that was set before the full requirements of the system were known.

Phased planning is a realistic approach that permits the project manager to plan only to the level of detail that is known at the time. Using this approach, the output of each phase of a project includes two planning documents: a *phase plan* and a *project plan*. The phase plan is prepared at the task or work package level and provides the detailed work that will be done in the next phase of the project (see the section in Chapter Four on Work Breakdown Structures for a definition of the terms *task* and *work package*).

The project plan is the overall plan for the remainder of the project, specifying anticipated completion date, estimated resources needed, and cost to complete the project.

Phased planning, in its broadest sense, may not be acceptable in some environments. It is often necessary to impose a deadline on a project before it starts. The customer needs to be in the building by a certain date. The book is to be published and released at the time a movie comes out in the hope that the book will "piggy back" on the anticipated success of the movie. (The author of *Karate for Kids* did just this to piggy-back on the movie *The Karate Kid*.)

However, even when the deadline is imposed, phased planning is still a useful approach. In fact, it bears out the first rule which must be learned in project planning.

The first rule of planning is to be prepared to *re*-plan.

Project Planning Steps

The basic planning steps and the resulting documents which must be generated are as follows:

Figure 2.2

Recognizing open-ended
problems

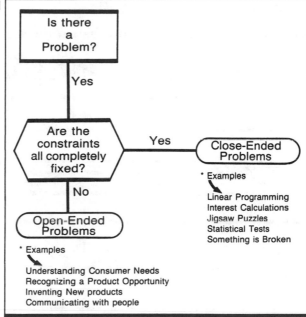

(Adapted from Rickards: see reading list.)

- Define the problem to be solved by the project.
- Develop a Work Breakdown Structure (WBS).
- Using the WBS, estimate activity durations, resource requirements, and costs (as appropriate for your environment).
- Prepare the project master schedule and budget.
- Decide on the project organization structure—whether matrix or hierarchical.
- Set up the project notebook.
- Get the plan signed off by all project stakeholders. (A sample signoff form is shown in Figure 2.3.)

A General Model of Project Management

Figure 2.4 shows a flow chart illustrating the overall approach to managing a project. Each step in the process is numbered, and the following discussion refers to step numbers as shown in the figure.

Figure 2.3

Project Plan Approval
Form

Project Plan Approval				
Project Description			Project Code	Date
From			Department	Return By
Your signature below indicates that you agree with the plan submitted, so far as your interests are concerned.				
	Approving Individual		Signed	Date
Functional Managers				
Directors				
President				
Project Manager				
Customers				
Comments				

Figure 2.4

A General Model of
Project Management

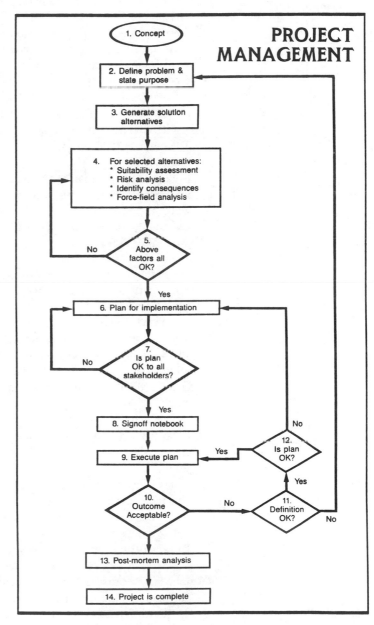

1. Step One is the concept phase of the project, in which someone identifies a need for a product or service. As was discussed in Chapter One, the definition of the problem to be solved is very sketchy at this point.
2. Step Two requires the planner to define the problem to be solved and state the purpose of the project. While this book does not cover the project selection process, in most organizations a cost-benefit trade-off analysis would be made to determine if the project meets a legitimate need and if it will provide a suitable return on the organization's investment. The purpose statement would assist in conducting that analysis.
3. In Step Three alternative approaches to doing the work are examined. This is an appropriate point at which to apply brainstorming or some other idea-generating process. At this point the selection of project *strategy* takes place.
4. Steps Four and Five involve the assessment of various strategies to determine if they are acceptable. Will a particular approach meet *good-fast-cheap* targets? Do we have the capability to implement this approach? What could go wrong (risk analysis)? Are there any unintended consequences of following this approach that we cannot live with? For example, in solving one problem, have we created another? Given the culture of this organization, will this approach be accepted by all members, especially upper management?
5. If the answer(s) to any question in Step Four is "no," then another alternative must be selected for evaluation.
6. In this step a detailed working plan is developed. This includes the Work Breakdown Structure, working schedule, organization structure, control system, and so on.
7. The signoff meeting is held in Step Seven. If the plan is not acceptable to stakeholders, replanning is done until a satisfactory plan is developed.
8. The plan is signed off (actually part of Step Seven, but shown separately to indicate its importance).

9. Implementation of the plan proceeds in Step Nine.
10. Progress is compared to the plan. If no deviation-from-plan is noted, eventually the work is completed successfully. On the other hand, if the outcome is not acceptable, move to Step Eleven.
11. Is the definition of the problem okay? If not, you must start over by going back to Step Two. If the definition is okay, then the plan must be examined.
12. Is the plan okay? If not, go back to Step Six and re-plan. If it is, then go to Step Nine and follow the plan as written. Note that if the plan is okay and the outcome is not acceptable, then the plan is not being followed. This will probably happen because insufficient resources are available to do the work as planned. If they are not obtainable, then it may be necessary to replan the project.
13. At each milestone, a post-mortem should be conducted so you can learn as you go. What did we do well in previous steps? What could stand improvement?
14. When the project is complete, the notebook is placed in a central file so that all members of the organization can have access to it for use in future planning.

Key Points

- If you have no plan, control is impossible!

- The people who must execute a plan should be involved in its preparation.

- Use a project notebook to fully document a project.

- The project plan should be signed off by stakeholders in a meeting, not through the mail.

- When significant changes to the plan are required, they are signed off by affected stakeholders.

- A stakeholder is anyone who has a vested interest in the project.

- Watch out for scope creep!

- Conduct a SWOT analysis during the planning stage.

- Define the problem to be solved before developing an implementation plan.

- Phased planning recognizes that planners do not have 20/20 foresight.

- Follow the project management flowchart.

CHAPTER 3 Defining Your Mission, Goals, and Objectives

The Mission Identification Process[1]

Before deciding on specific goals and objectives that the project team must accomplish, it is important that team members decide on their "reason for being." This is called the team's mission, and it may remain constant throughout the life of the project or it may change. For most teams, it is advisable to reexamine the mission statement at least once a year to determine if it has or should change, although this probably will not be true for a project team.

Because mission statements have been misused and abused, many people hold them in very low regard. Nevertheless, a mission statement is invaluable when properly used. In fact, like so many things, it is not the mission statement that is of no value but the fact that *no value is placed on it* that is the problem.

Once the mission statement is developed, it should be *used.* This seems obvious, yet many organizations seem to forget the mission statement after it is written. Perhaps it is because they go into the firefighting mode and forget their mission. Like the old joke, they have forgotten that the objective was to drain the swamp, because they have been too busy fighting the alligators.

In any case, the mission statement should be used to set goals and objectives, to make decisions and to provide the goods and services the organization has determined it should be providing to meet the needs of customers.

A mission statement should answer three questions:

1. What do we do?
2. For whom do we do it?
3. How do we go about it?

Before these questions can be answered, it is useful for the team to work through a process in which they answer a number of questions. Table 3.1 lists the questions which should be answered before attempting to write the mission statement

Note that the process of writing a mission statement involves identifying stakeholders, among whom are your *customers,* and that you are supposed to list what customers want from you. I suggest that team members not try to answer this by themselves. Rather, ask the customer!

There are too many examples in this country of products and services being provided without asking the customer what he or she wants. It is only by satisfying the needs of the customer that a project team will succeed.

To highlight the importance of satisfying the customer, I recently saw a list of the eight characteristics which were determined through a world-wide survey to make for the most effective organizations. The first two are enlightening. They are:

- Empowerment of employees.
- Delighting the customer.

Empowering employees will be discussed in Chapter Nine, but note the second characteristic. How long has it been since you, as a customer, have been delighted with the product or service provided to you by an organization? As someone has said, if it is true that we are becoming a service economy, we are in trouble, because we give such poor service in general. Think for a moment about what you want from an organization when you are a customer. The following list is fairly representative of what most people want as customers:

What I want as a customer:

- To be provided products and services that have high quality at a reasonable price.
- To have my needs met.
- To be treated with respect.

Table 3.1

The Mission Identification
Process

- Identify the team's *internal* and *external* environment.
- List all of the team's *stakeholders*.
- Highlight the team's *customers* from within the list of stakeholders just generated.
- Check the three most important stakeholders—at least one of them should be the team's major customer.
- Make a list of those things your three most important stakeholders want from the team.
- When the team has finished its job, how will members know they were successful? List those *criteria for success* which will be used to judge the team's performance.
- What critical events might occur in the future that could affect the team's success either positively or negatively?
- Now write the mission and purpose statement.

Figure 3.1

Primary Mission
Procedure

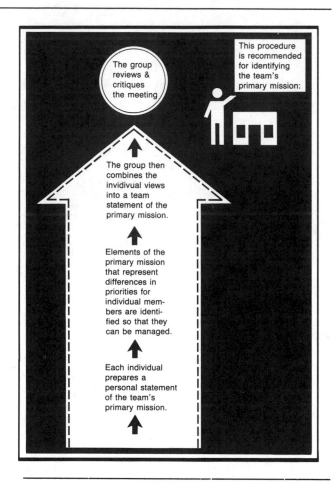

The last step in Table 3.1 is to write the mission and purpose statement for the team. The procedure shown in Figure 3.1 is recommended for identifying the team's primary mission.

An Example of a
Mission Statement[2]

Project Management Institute is the professional society for project managers. Their mission is:

> To be the leading recognized professional and technical association in advancing the state of the art of pro-

gram and project management. To be achieved through the development and dissemination of the theory and practice of effective management of resources in reaching project goals.

Setting Project Objectives

Once a satisfactory definition of the project has been developed and a mission statement has been written, it is time to decide what must be done. In my opinion, all project objectives should be in writing. There are at least two reasons for this.

The Importance of Objectives

One reason is that the process of writing them out forces you to clarify them. Often, when we carry an objective around in our heads, it is not even really clear to ourselves, much less anyone else. Secondly, by putting objectives in writing, all members of the project team can have access to them so that nothing is forgotten. Following are several reasons why objectives should be established in a project in the first place.

1. Unity of action is more likely to occur when there is pursuit of a common objective. (See Figure 3.2.)

    To be most effective as a manager, it is helpful to think of your job as being to meet organization (project) objectives while helping members of the project team to simultaneously meet their own objectives. In this way you build commitment to the project effort, which is ultimately going to produce *alignment* of team members with the overall direction in which the project is going, which is naturally necessary for success.
2. The greater the *participation* in setting meaningful work objectives with *accountability* for the result, the greater the motivation for completing them. This does not mean that total participation is required in managing a project. It only means that when it is practical, members of the team will be more committed to objectives when they have a hand in setting them.
3. Finally, progress can only be measured in terms of what one is trying to make progress toward. Thus,

Figure 3.2

Project Effort

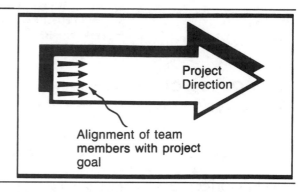

Project
Direction

Alignment of team
members with project
goal

objectives give you a target toward which to move
and allow you to measure progress as you go along.
Remember, if you don't know where you're going,
how will you know when you get there?

Kinds of Project Objectives

Objectives may be to:

- Develop expertise in some area.
- Become competitive.
- Improve productivity.
- Improve quality.
- Reduce costs.
- Modify an existing facility.
- Develop a new sales strategy.
- Develop a new product.

Criteria for Sound Objectives

By complying with the following guidelines, it should
be possible to develop clear objectives for which
specific implementation steps can be worked out, and
using them should enable individuals to tell when they
have achieved the desired result.

- A statement of objective should be *specific*—that is,
  not a fuzzy, vague statement, such as "I want to be
  the best." What does that mean? In fact, as I define
  them, the difference between a goal and an objective
  is based on how specific it is. To me, a goal is
  broader and less specific than an objective. However, there is no universal agreement about this defi-

nition, so you may find other authors reversing the meanings of the terms. All that really matters is that you understand the definition being used.

- They should be *measurable* when possible. This can be very difficult to achieve. How do you measure performance improvement of knowledge workers, for example?

   In the event that the objective is not quantifiable, then some qualitative evidence must be used. In other words, how will you know you achieved the objective unless there is some evidence or criteria that can be used. For quantifiable objectives, see Table 3.2 for units that can be used in measuring targets.

- They should fit *higher level* organization objectives. In terms of projects, this means that the objectives set by functional groups should support the attainment of the overall project objectives. In turn, projects are chosen such that overall organization targets will be reached.

- They should be stated in terms of *deliverable items*, if possible. Deliverable items may be assessment reports, written recommendations, etc. In any case, a deliverable is something tangible and is very useful as a measure of whether a milestone has been met. For example, a milestone might be to complete a design; if the deliverable is a drawing of that design, then accomplishment of the milestone is much easier to gauge.

- They must be *comprehensible*—that is, stated in such a way that other people will understand what you are trying to achieve. Failure to understand the objective is often the cause of major problems in organizations. If I were going to vote for which one of the criteria is most important, I would vote for this one!

- They should be *time-limited* if possible. This is usually not a problem in project environments, where schedule is very important. However, it is helpful to remember this rule when setting performance-improvement objectives for employees. If such objectives are not time-limited, they will never happen!

- When several objectives must be met before another can be achieved, it is useful to *prioritize* them using the steps to be discussed later in this chapter.
- When appropriate, objectives should be assigned a *risk factor* so others in the organization will be aware of such risk.
- The statement should say *what* is to be accomplished, but not how to do it. The *how* component should be reserved for problem-solving. The objective, in other words, specifies that we want to get from point A to point B without saying how to do so.
- The objective should be *attainable*. Setting unrealistic objectives only causes people to have no commitment to them. A *stretch* objective is fine, so long as it is not totally out of reach.
- They should also specify a *single* end result. When multiple objectives are combined into one statement, it becomes difficult to sort out what is being said.

I have found the following two questions to be useful both in setting objectives and in monitoring progress toward those objectives:

- What is the desired outcome? This is called the *outcome frame* and helps keep people focused on the result they are trying to achieve, rather than on the effort being expended to get there.
- How will we know when we achieve it? I call this the *evidence* question. For those objectives which

Table 3.2

Measures for Objectives

Dimensions to Use to Quantify Objectives

Time units	Phases
Frequency rates	Percentiles
Ratios	Quartiles
Index numbers	Deciles
Percentages	Mean deviations
Averages	Correlations
Number aggregates	Volume amounts
Degrees	Units of production

are qualitative in nature, it forces you to think about how you will know that the objective has been accomplished.

Examples of Pitfalls in Writing Objectives

Even though the criteria for sound objectives are fairly specific, it is still easy to make some errors in writing your own statements. Following are some examples of statements which could be improved.

- The objective is to achieve a 12-percent Return On Investment within 18 months.

One problem with such a statement is that it has no real deadline. A few months from the time it is written, you are likely to forget when you started, and therefore can't remember when you should have achieved the desired outcome.

While it is true that you may have to put a time-frame on the objective initially because it is contingent on something else taking place, as soon as possible, put a real deadline on it.

The other factor which may be a problem with this objective is that the amount of the investment is not specified. For that reason, it is hard to judge whether it is feasible or not. A 12-percent return on a $100,000 investment is more likely to be attainable than for a $100 investment.

- Complete the design of a new prototype in twelve months within a cost of $100,000 and without farm-out of work to other vendors.

This objective also should be deadlined in its final form. Note, however, that it has a constraint. It does not tell how the objective is to be achieved, but it is desired to conduct all work internally, rather than giving the work to another vendor. Constraints such as this one are legitimate.

- Reduce weld rejects in frame assembly from 2 percent to 0.5 percent by June 1, while holding cost of welds to $1.50 or less.

It could be argued that this objective has tied down *good, fast,* and *cheap* simultaneously, thus violating the rule that only two of them can be specified at a time. However, the cost target has flexibility. The statement says that any cost less-than or equal-to $1.50 is acceptable. Establishing a boundary on cost, so long as it is practical to achieve the objective for that figure, is generally acceptable.

• Read twelve new books on management by December 31 of this year at the rate of one per month.

This one has a guideline built in to prevent the individual from waiting until December to read all twelve books!

You should spend time writing out some of the objectives you are trying to achieve, applying the rules above. As a test on how sound they are, have someone else read them for clarity, and revise them as necessary.

Conducting a SWOT Analysis

Once objectives have been specified, it is useful to do a SWOT analysis to determine where you may have to apply special efforts in order to achieve the desired outcome. The form in Figure 3.3 has been designed to help you with this.

The form in Figure 3.4 is an example of how all project objectives might be listed and assigned numbers and code words so that they can be discussed in "shorthand" form. These forms should be in the project notebook.

Establishing Priorities

In every organization, there is always more work to be done than the organization can accomplish with its limited resources. This means that priorities must be established so that work will be done to achieve the best use of those limited resources. These objectives are ordered based on value to the organization.[3]

Factors that may affect the priority of an objective include customer pressures, market forces, cost considerations and the like. Objectives influenced by such

Figure 3.3

SWOT Analysis Form

© 1990 by James P. Lewis

*SWOT analysis-
goals &
objectives*

STATEMENT OF
GOAL/OBJECTIVE

LIST STRENGTHS	HOW CAN YOU BEST TAKE ADVANTAGE OF THESE?	LIST WEAKNESSES	HOW CAN YOU MINIMIZE THE IMPACT OF THESE?
WHAT OPPORTUNITIES DOES THIS PROJECT PRESENT?	HOW CAN YOU BEST TAKE ADVANTAGE OF THEM?	LIST THREATS: those risks or obstacles that might prevent success	HOW CAN YOU DEAL WITH EACH IDENTIFIED THREAT?

Figure 3.4

Project Objectives Form

project objectives		Date _____ Page _____ of _____
Project		
Obj. No.	Keyword	Statement of Objective
Comments		

factors must be rank-ordered taking all such variables into consideration. Generally it is fairly easy to determine the most and least important objectives, but those in-between are more difficult to rank.

It may be enough to simply list objectives and then group them into categories A, B, and C—with A being most important, etc. On the other hand, it may be necessary to actually rank-order the list. When this is done for more than ten objectives, the task becomes formidable. To make the process easier, first group them into A, B, and C categories, then use the method of paired comparisons to rank within categories. As an example of this, consider the following eight objectives. Note that at this point no dates have been assigned.

A similar result could have been obtained using the ranking matrix shown in Figure 3.5. For this matrix, objectives are listed down the left and across the top, and are then considered by working across one row at a time, answering the questions on the sides of the matrix. For example, in the first row, if the question is asked, "Is Objective 1 more important than 2," the answer is "yes," so a 1 is placed in the cell below column 2. For Objective 1 compared to 3, however, the answer is "no," so a zero is placed in the cell below column 3.

Once a row has been filled in, the column of the same number should be filled in with the *inverse* of the row. That is, if a cell in the row contains a 1, then enter a zero into the corresponding cell in the column. Following this rule, column 1 is filled in with the inverse of row 1. Note that this rule only applies to cells below the diagonal, since those above the diagonal will be filled in as the rows are worked through.

When all cells have been filled in, each row is totalled. The row with the highest total is rank one, and so on. If there is a tie between two rows, simply look inside the matrix to determine the ranking, since it has already been specified. In other words, if rows 3 and 5 were tied, you would look inside the matrix to see if Objective 3 is more important than Objective 5, since that has already been determined.

Business Improvement Project

List of objectives:

1. Penetrate the Southwestern market.
2. Develop new WIDGET.
3. Hire new sales manager.
4. Move into new office facility.
5. Bring level of cash reserves up to $200,000.
6. Open an office in London.
7. Conduct a survey of all products competitive with new WIDGET.
8. Hold class on Quality Improvement for all managers.

For this list of objectives, the business manager has decided that objectives should be grouped into categories as follows:

A:	1	3	5
B:	2	7	8
C:	4	6	

Now that this grouping has been done, the manager might fairly easily be able to rank the objectives in each category, as follows:

A	B	C
5	7	6
3	2	4
1	8	

Thus, the rank ordering for his list is now:

RANK	OBJECTIVE
1.	5
2.	3
3.	1
4.	7
5.	2
6.	8
7.	6
8.	4

Figure 3.5

Ranking Matrix

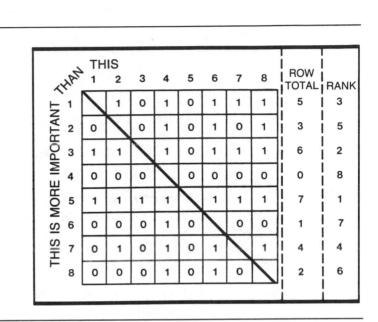

Key Points

- A mission statement should be developed for larger projects, before goals and objectives are established.

- A mission statement should be used as a guide to make decisions in the project.

- Satisfying the customer(s) of a project must be a primary concern.

- Objectives should be written out and placed in the project notebook.

- Objectives should be written following the criteria specified in the chapter.

- Objectives should contain actual calendar deadlines, rather than being specified as "within so many months."

- A SWOT analysis should be conducted as part of the planning process.

- Priorities can be established using the priority matrix.

CHAPTER 4 Estimating Time, Cost, and Resources

As mentioned at the beginning of this book, back around 2600 B.C. pharaoh Zoser called the priest-engineer Imhotep to the palace and presented him with a new project.

"Imhotep," the pharaoh began, "I have decided to erect a monument to commemorate my accomplishments, and it will also be my tomb. I want it built something like this."

He handed Imhotep a sketch drawn on papyrus of a colossal pyramid. Imhotep examined the sketch and felt his stomach draw up in a knot. He knew what was coming next.

"It is a magnificent structure, lord," he said. "What do you wish of me?"

Figure 4.1

Pyramids

"I want you to build it, Imhotep. You are the best priest-engineer in my kingdom. But I need to know two things. What will it cost me and how long will it take?"

Imhotep felt his mouth get dry, while his palms began sweating. How was he to answer the pharaoh's question? In the history of mankind, there had never been a structure such as this built (Figure 4.1).

"I will need some time to answer these questions, majesty," he replied slowly.

"Let me know next week," the pharaoh replied. "I want to get started on this as soon as possible. And I need to know if we must pillage some of our neighbors to raise money and collect some slave workers."

"I'll get right on it, lord," Imhotep answered.

* * *

Every project manager since Imhotep's time has been faced with a similar problem. How do you estimate what it will take to do something? (See Figure 4.2.) After the first pyramid was built, estimating what it would take to build the next one was easier. But that does not mean that an exact determination of time, cost, and resources could be given. It would still be an *estimate*, and an estimate is *not exact!*

Estimating is never simple, and the higher the stakes, the more anxiety-provoking the job is. However, unless the estimating problem can be managed, projects will never come in on time or on budget..

How does a project manager know how long it will take to do a project, even given that he or she knows how many human resources are available to do the work? The answer, of course, is *experience!*

Figure 4.2

Estimating Problem

How Do You
Estimate
What It Will Take
To Do
Something?

Unless the estimating
problem can be managed,
projects will never come in
on time or on budget!

After Zoser built the first pyramid, estimating the next one was easier, but not exact. But by the time several pyramids had been built, the estimates became more accurate. Then along came the Sphinx, something very different than the others! Do you suppose the project manager for the Sphinx had some difficulty estimating that job? Undoubtedly he did.

In any case, let us examine what we mean by experience and its relationship to estimating activity durations. For example, if you have been driving to the same workplace from the same home for several years, using the same route each time, you know about how

Table 4.1

Driving Times for
Metropolitan Workers

Average time:	45 minutes
Shortest time:	35 minutes
Longest time:	60 minutes*

*Assuming no blizzards, etc.

long it takes to get to work. In large metropolitan areas, people report times like those shown in Table 4.1.

When asked, "What is your best estimate of how long it will take you to get to work tomorrow?" they usually respond with, "forty-five minutes." That is, they give the average driving time.

However, if you ask, "How long would you allow yourself to get to work, if you absolutely had to get there on time?" they say, "one hour." So they allow themselves the upper limit, just in case they are faced with a wreck or whatever causes their time to go to the upper limit. That way, they will be sure to get to work on time, unless the situation is extreme and the time exceeds the one-hour upper limit.

In a project, much the same process is involved. If a task has been performed a large number of times, the average duration is known, given a certain level of human resources to do the work, and this average can be used as the basis for an estimate.

There is only one difficulty. From statistics, we know that an average duration has only a 50/50 likelihood of occurring (See Figure 4.3.).[1] That is, there is a 50-percent chance that it will take longer than the average duration and also a 50-percent chance that it could take less than the average.[2] Having a 50-percent chance of success in completing one's work is not very comforting, especially if the stakes are high and the organization is determined to have the project completed by some predetermined date.

It is for this reason that people are inclined to pad their estimates. As the normal distribution curve in Figure 4.3 shows, there is an 84 percent probability that a duration one standard deviation above the mean can be

Figure 4.3

Normal Distribution Curve

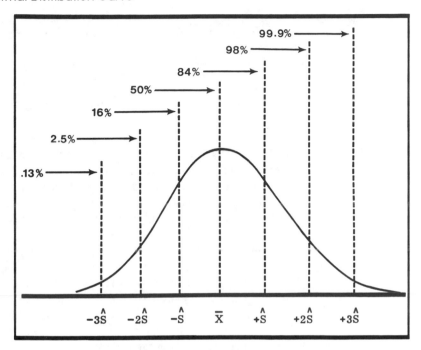

met, 98 percent for two standard deviations, and 99.9 percent for three standard deviations. Thus, by padding, the project manager can greatly increase the probability that the work can be completed in the estimated time.

Unfortunately, safety carries a price. While increasing the allowed time increases the probability of a successful scheduled completion, it also increases the budgeted cost of the project, possibly to the point where the job will not be funded.

For this reason, one of the assumptions made in project estimating is that *average durations* are used, unless specified otherwise. The idea is that, for a project consisting of a large number of activities, some of the work will take longer than the average estimated duration, while other tasks will take less than the average, so that the total project completion time will gravitate toward the mean expected time for the critical path!

> Of course, Murphy's Law seems to prevent such an occurrence.

While padding is certainly justified to reduce risk, my opinion is that it must be done above-board, on a task-by-task basis. Otherwise, the project manager might incorrectly assume that every member of the team has provided average-duration estimates. The manager then puts some padding into the project at the top level, thus adding "fat" to that which individuals have already put into their estimates, and the project is then sure to be too expensive.

This is one reason for not getting into game-playing in an organization. It sometimes happens that a manager asks for an estimate, and when it is provided, the manager cuts the estimate by 10 or 15 percent, based on the belief that the estimate contains at least that much "fat." Note that the probability of achieving a time one standard deviation below the mean is only 16 percent, so cutting an estimate that was an average-expectedduration severely reduces the probability that the time can be met.

If the project manager gets burned because his estimates were averages and they were cut, then the next time he is asked for an estimate, he will indeed pad, since he expects that his estimate will be cut. This time, however, the manager cuts 20 percent, so the next time the project manager pads 25 percent, and so on. Such "games" are hardly productive.

The objective of all project planning should be to develop a plan that is *realistic*, so that managers can accurately assess the feasibility of the work. The objective should not be to try to "get" the project manager by holding him or her accountable to unrealistic deadlines.[3]

It is instructive to consider the cause of variations in working times, using the driving example as a guide.

Suppose we agree that the time it takes to drive to work varies widely because of unpredictable traffic-flow patterns. If we could eliminate those, then the variation in driving time could be greatly reduced.

Indeed, suppose there were absolutely no other traffic on the road than the single driver. (Perhaps this can be accomplished by leaving very early in the morning, before other drivers get out on the road.) In that case, there should be no variation in driving time—right? Of course that is not true. Even though the variation would be reduced, no driver can maintain an exactly constant speed, or even the exact-same variation at the same point in the road day after day.

For this reason, there will always be some variation in working times, caused by factors outside the control of the operator! It is therefore unrealistic to expect that anyone can estimate precisely how long a task will take to complete. (As someone has said, anyone who has 20/20 precision in forecasting should leave project management and invest in the stock market. The returns would be far greater than anyone could make managing projects.)

Other Factors in Estimating

An average-expected-duration for an activity can only be developed by assuming that the work will be nearly identical to work previously done and that the person(s) being assigned to the task will have a certain skill level. If a less-skilled person is assigned to the work, it can be expected to take longer, and conversely, a more-skilled person could probably do the job faster. Thus, adjustments must be made for experience or skill of the resource assigned to the task.

However, we also know that there is no *exact* correlation between experience and speed of doing work. It may not always be true that the more experienced person can do the job faster than the person with less experience. And putting pressure on the individual will pay dividends only up to a point. I remember once when I was pressuring one of my project team members to get a job done faster, and he got fed up with the pressure. Finally, he said, "Putting two jockeys on one horse won't make him run any faster." And he was right.

Then there was a project manager who told me that when his boss doesn't like an estimate of how long it will take to perform a task, he tells him to *use a more productive person!* That was his solution to all scheduling problems. (See Figure 4.4.)

Another factor is how much productive time the person will apply to the task each day. It is not uncommon in some organizations for people to spend an average of 25 percent of each day in meetings, on the phone, waiting for supplies and other activities, all of which reduce the time available to spend on project work. Allowances must be made for such non-project time.

In addition, if experience with a task is minimal, the expected duration might be adjusted upward, compared to the closest task for which experience exists. If virtually no experience can be used as a basis for estimating, then it might be appropriate to use PERT techniques (see Chapter Eight). Another possibility is to use DELPHI or some other estimating method. For an application of DELPHI method to project estimating, consult the book by Burrill and Ellsworth cited in the reading list.

For construction projects, there are books available containing *means tables,* which list the average expected durations for typical construction activities, together with "fudge factors" to be used in adjusting those times to compensate for geographic location, weather, and other factors.

For other types of projects, unfortunately, there are no means tables available, so historical data must be developed by keeping records on previous project work. This is, perhaps, one of the most important benefits of developing a standardized project management methodology—by doing the work in specified ways and by keeping records on actual working times, an organization can develop a data base which can be used to greatly improve future project estimates.

Figure 4.4

More Productive Person

Developing and Using the Work Breakdown Structure

In the previous text, the terms *project* and *activity* were used more-or-less interchangeably to discuss estimating. However, it should be clear that estimating the duration of a single task is much easier than estimating the duration of a project, which consists of a multitude of tasks.

This is not to say that top-level estimates are not made. If a "quick-and-dirty" estimate is needed so that a decision can be made as to whether a project should be done in the first place, it would not be out of line to make a project-level estimate by simply comparing the anticipated project to a former one and adjusting accordingly for any obvious differences.

Such estimates have very large tolerances, of course. The actual cost might vary as much as ± 50 to 75 percent from the estimate. (More realistically, the costs might vary -10 percent to +100 percent in such cases. The tolerances are seldom symmetrical.)

If a greater degree of estimating accuracy is needed, the work must be broken down into smaller increments, or tasks, each of which can be estimated with relatively good accuracy. Once task-level estimates have been made, they can be combined to give a total project estimate. This idea is the heart of the Work Breakdown Structure (WBS).

Once a project definition has been completed and objectives have been written, development of the WBS can proceed. If defining the project is the most important step in managing a project, developing the WBS is the next-most important step in the planning process, since it provides a framework in which to accomplish the following:

- All tasks to be performed can be identified and resources allocated to them.
- Once resource levels have been allocated to tasks, estimates of task durations can be made.
- All costs and resource allocations can be totalled to develop the overall project budget.
- Task durations can then be used in developing a working schedule for the project.
- Performance can be tracked against these identified cost, schedule and resource allocations.
- Assignment of responsibility for each element can be made.

One common WBS is a six-level indented one, which names each level as shown in Figure 4.5.

The six-level structure is not the only possibility, of course. Organizations that do very large projects, such as construction of power-generating plants, may use a structure with 10 to 12 levels. A rule-of-thumb is that no more than 20 levels should be used, no matter how large the project.

The six-level structure shown in Figure 4.5 begins at the program level. The difference between programs and projects is, then, simply a matter of magnitude. A manager who supervises a number of project managers would be called a *program manager*, based on this notation scheme.

An example of a program would be the development of the space shuttle. There were numerous projects involved in developing the shuttle. Such things as designing the heating and air-conditioning system, the guidance and navigation system, and so on, were projects in their own right. Many of those projects were done by contractors and the program manager was re-

Figure 4.5

Names for WBS Levels

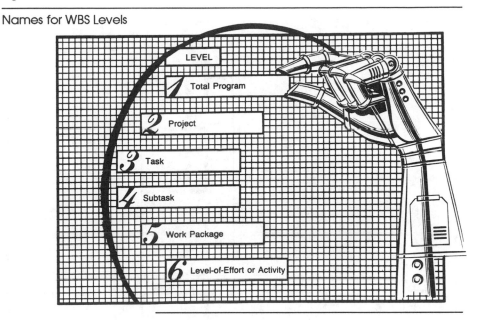

sponsible for ensuring that when all of the components were integrated, they worked in concert.

To illustrate the use of the WBS, Figure 4.6 shows a partial six-level WBS for a weekend home maintenance project. (Only part of the tasks have been shown, in order to keep the diagram to manageable size.)

Note that it begins at the project level, rather than the program level. When only projects are involved, this is the conventional use of the WBS.

As is shown by the WBS, under the task called *Paint Inside* there are four subtasks, called *move furniture, cover floors, mask windows,* and *paint*. In actually doing the work, it would be necessary to move furniture before the floors could be covered, and that would have to be done before painting begins, but masking windows might be done in parallel with furniture moving and floor covering. However, all four subtasks must be done to have accomplished the task called *Paint Inside*.

This illustrates an important point in developing a WBS: do not attempt to show sequencing of work with the WBS—that is done in developing the schedule. Fur-

Figure 4.6

WBS for Home Project

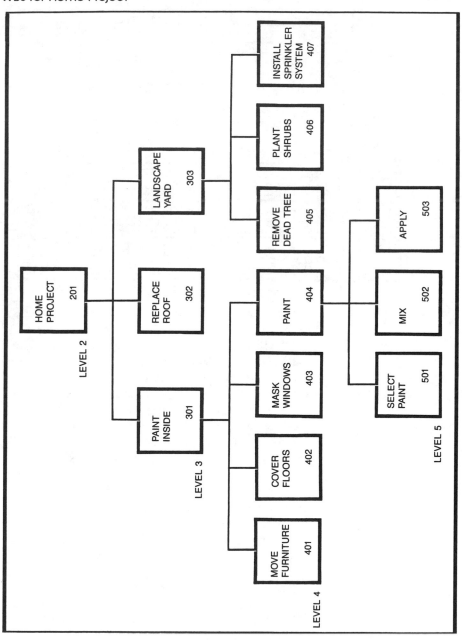

ther, not all "legs" or branches of the WBS need to be broken down to level six. The working rule is that a path will be broken down to a level sufficient to estimate to the degree of accuracy required. It might be possible to stop at level four for one path, while another might have to be extended to level six in order to attain the same accuracy.

Working Rule

> Do not attempt to show activity sequencing with a Work Breakdown Structure.

As a practical matter, the procedure for developing a WBS is fairly straightforward. You simply ask the question, "What will have to be done in order to accomplish...?" In the home maintenance example, the individual planning this project would begin by asking what maintenance is required for the house. The roof needs to be replaced. That will be a major task. The inside must be painted— another task. Finally, the yard needs to be landscaped, which is a final task.

For the painting task, what must be done to accomplish it? Those subtasks were discussed previously. When they have been identified, the question can be asked again for each of them, producing the level-five work packages. Then these can be subdivided, until level six is reached. It may be that some paths will stop at level four or five simply because a point is reached where the work cannot be further subdivided. On the other hand, it may be necessary to go beyond six levels, in which case the planner will have to develop his or her own terms for the additional levels.

Rule

> Break down the work only as far as needed to develop an estimate to the required degree of accuracy.

In any case, once a suitable level has been reached, estimates of activity durations can be developed, resources assigned, and cost estimates can be determined for the work. For example, if an activity will require 10 hours of work, and labor is expected to cost $12.00 per hour, the activity will cost $120 (See Figure 4.7.)

If costs are developed for each work package, those which combine to make a subtask can be added up to obtain the subtask cost. These can then be combined to develop a task cost, and so on, until total project cost has been calculated. See Figure 4.8.

Estimating Accuracy Using the WBS

Earlier we saw that estimating project costs at the project level can yield budgets which have fairly large tolerances. Typical figures are -10 percent to +100 percent. If work is broken down to level six, those tolerances might be reduced to as little as ± 3 percent for very well-defined construction projects, or around ± 15 percent for others, such as research and development.

As an example of how uncertainty affects estimating tolerances, suppose you were asked how long it would take and how much it would cost to develop an AIDS vaccine. Already work has been going on for a number of years, with no end in sight.

Figure 4.7

Work Package Estimate

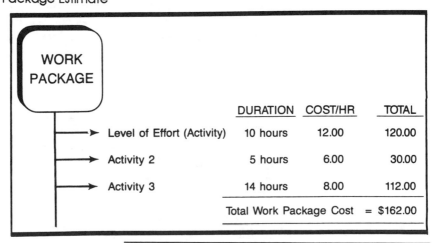

	DURATION	COST/HR	TOTAL
Level of Effort (Activity)	10 hours	12.00	120.00
Activity 2	5 hours	6.00	30.00
Activity 3	14 hours	8.00	112.00
	Total Work Package Cost	=	$162.00

Figure 4.8

Cost Estimates

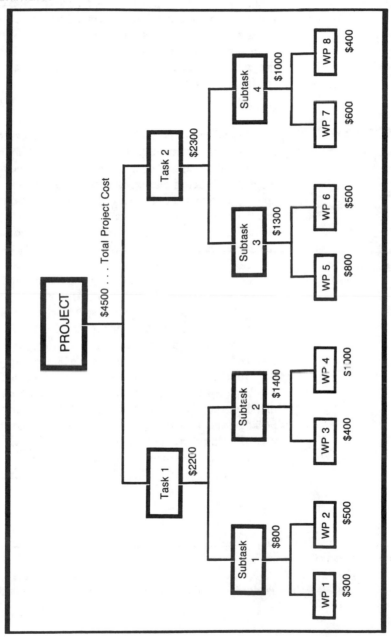

Using the WBS to Show Project Scope

One additional benefit of the WBS is that it provides a visual representation of the total scope of the project. It is not uncommon for project managers to develop cost and duration estimates for a project, only to have someone ask, "How can it cost so much?" Having a WBS in hand, it becomes easier to show others the total magnitude and complexity of the work involved, so they can see first-hand why it costs so much.

The Chart-of-Accounts

Once a project has been planned, it will be necessary to track progress against the plan, so that control can be exercised and so some indication can be given of how well the project is being managed. In most organizations, computers are used to collect and report data on costs and work expended. That data is usually collected by assigning charges to certain cost accounting categories, defined by a *chart-of-accounts* system.

However, many organizations have such chart-of-accounts systems only for tracking manufacturing labor, but not project work. In such a case, if it is desired to track labor applied to a project, a special chart-of-accounts must be set up. A sample is shown in Figure 4.9.

Note that if a number is assigned to a project, say 201, and also to a work package, say 578, then work on that work package could be specified as shown in Table 4.2. By referring to the chart-of-accounts, you can see that draft specifications were prepared for the work package, and 37 hours of labor were expended on the task. By comparing the *actual hours worked* to the *planned hours,* the manager can see if the project is progressing satisfactorily. This will be discussed in more detail in Chapter Nine.

Table 4.2

Tracking Labor on a Work Package

Project	Work Package	Account	Hours Worked
201	578	012	37

Figure 4.9

Sample
Chart-of-Accounts for
Project Accounting

Account Number	Activity Description	Account Number	Activity Description
000 *		032	Camera work
001	Development of concepts	033	Office layout
002	Preliminary design	034	Reserved
003	Computer analysis	035	Reserved
004	Environmental tests	036	Contract administration
005	Alternative selection	037	Contractor payroll certification
006	Delphi technique		
007	Systems analysis	038	Reserved
008	Reserved	039	Reserved
009	Field investigation	070 *	
010 *		071	Project management
011	Final design	072	Project planning & scheduling
012	Draft specifications		
013	Drafting/graphics	073	Project coordination
014	Checking drawings	074	Reserved
015	Specifications review	075	Client meetings & conferences
016	Maintenance work		
017	Technical writing	076	Public meetings & hearings
018	Cost estimating	077	Reserved
019	Bid preparation	078	Reserved
020 *		079	Project review meetings
021	Quality control checks	080 *	
022	Reserved	081	Administrative services
023	Reserved	082	Clerical support
024	Computer data preparation	083	Composing & editing
025	Computer analysis	084	Typing
026	Computer keypunching	085	Reproductions/printing
027	Reserved	086	Training
028	Shop drawing review	087	Marketing & sales
029	Reserved	088	Reserved
030 *		089	Reserved
031	Prepare visual aids	090 *	

In the planning stage, the chart-of-accounts can also be very useful as a checklist. One of the greatest aids of a WBS is to ensure that no work has been overlooked in the project. Horror stories abound detailing what happens when significant work is overlooked in the planning stage.

One project manager told me about a construction job which was supposed to cost about two million dollars, except the planners forgot the site preparation work—that is, all of the land excavation. By the time the oversight was discovered, they already had earth-moving equipment on site moving dirt around.

When they were told about the error, the clients' faces literally turned pale, but by then there was nothing they could do except absorb the added cost. They were already committed to do the job. The site preparation cost alone was nearly $600,000, increasing the total project cost by about 30 percent over the original estimate.

Estimating & Tracking Progress Using the Chart-of-Accounts

Using the chart-of-accounts together with the WBS makes it easy to develop forms like the Work Package Estimating form shown in Figure 4.10.

To track time, weekly time cards can be set up to record work applied to each work package, as shown in Figure 4.11. These cards can then be used to input data to the computer so that weekly charges against the project can be recorded, the cost of labor calculated, and reports sent to the project manager for comparison with the planned levels of work and cost.

One caution is in order about such time cards.[4] If people are allowed to fill them out at the end of each week, using only their memories as a guide, they are writing fiction! Virtually no one has such a good memory that he or she can tell you with accuracy what he or she worked on Monday a week ago.

This does not mean that we want to track work to the nearest fifteen minutes. However, with loaded labor costs (direct labor plus overhead) being as much as sixty dollars per hour, or a dollar each minute, it seems reasonable to expect accuracies to the nearest hour. Otherwise, comparing "made-up" numbers to the plan will tell nothing about what is really happening, and such fictitious data can hardly be used for future estimating of working times.

This means that contributors to a project must record their actual working times at least *daily*, if the

Figure 4.10

Work Package Estimate
Form

| WORK PACKAGE ESTIMATE | | | | | | |

Page _____ of _____
Date _____
Revision _____

Prepared by_____

Department _____

Program # _____ Description _____

Project # _____ Description _____

Work Pkg. # _____ Description _____

Acct. No.	Description of Activity	Responsible Individual	Time Req'd.	Time Units	Unit Cost	Total Cost

| | Work Package Total Cost This Page | |
| | TOTAL WORK PACKAGE COST | |

Notes		
Acct. No.	Inputs Required From	Date Req'd.

Figure 4.11

Time Card

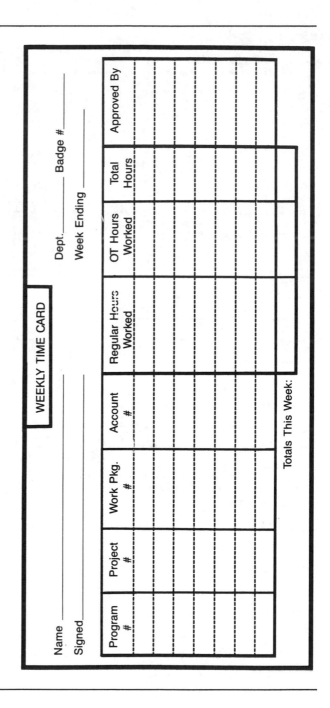

desired accuracy is to be achieved. Some of them will object that they are being treated like children when this requirement is enforced. The best counter-argument is to show them that it is ultimately for their benefit, since it will permit more accurate estimates in the future, no doubt reducing the amount of overtime they have to work because the original estimate was too low.

> Contributors to the project must record working times *daily*, or they are writing *fiction!*

Another problem that some organizations have is that salaried people (who usually do not get paid for overtime) are supposed to simply turn in a card that shows 40 total hours each week. (Which is sufficient for payroll purposes.) This is not very helpful for project accounting. If an individual actually worked 60 hours on the job, it is necessary to capture that actual time, so that the next time a similar activity is estimated, real figures are being used. This discrepancy between the needs of project tracking and payroll will either have to be resolved with the data processing department or else separate project records will have to be kept, which really is an inefficient way of doing it.

Linear Responsibility Charts

One rather common problem in larger projects is that people lose track of who is supposed to be working on what tasks. While the standard organization chart shows who reports to whom, it does not show relationships in a project. The linear responsibility chart is designed to do exactly that. The chart in Figure 4.12 shows in one horizontal line all team members involved in a work function, and the nature of their involvement. The vertical line shows all work in which a person is involved, together with the degree of his or her responsibility. The code numbers used are typical, but any coding scheme that fits your requirements can be used.

Figure 4.12

Linear Responsibility
Chart

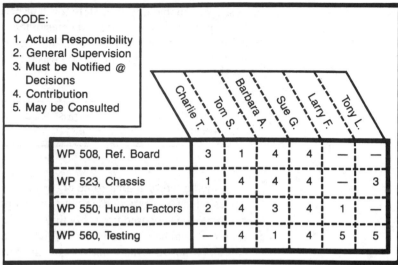

	Charlie T.	Tom S.	Barbara A.	Sue G.	Larry F.	Tony L.
WP 508, Ref. Board	3	1	4	4	—	—
WP 523, Chassis	1	4	4	4	—	3
WP 550, Human Factors	2	4	3	4	1	—
WP 560, Testing	—	4	1	4	5	5

CODE:

1. Actual Responsibility
2. General Supervision
3. Must be Notified @ Decisions
4. Contribution
5. May be Consulted

In the chart shown in Figure 4.12, Charlie T has actual responsibility for Work Package 523, the chassis. He is also providing some general supervision for Work Package 550 and must be notified about decisions affecting Work Package 508 (perhaps because changes to the Reference Board will affect his chassis design in some way).

A blank cell in the matrix indicates that the person is not involved in the work package. Most importantly: *no horizontal line can contain but a single "1," since two people cannot have ultimate responsibility for getting a job done.*

Key Points

- Estimates are based on experience, using the average expected time to perform a task.

- Padding is legitimate to reduce risk, but should be done *above board.*

- An estimate Is not a *fact!*

- Reduce time available for a person to work on a project to allow for meetings, breaks, and other interruptions.

- The WBS is used to develop estimates, assign personnel, track progress, and show scope of project work.

- Break work down only to the level needed to develop an estimate sufficiently accurate for the intended use.

- Use a chart-of-accounts to track labor costs.

- To ensure accuracy, time worked on the project should be recorded daily.

- Use a linear responsibility chart to show who is responsible for various activities in a project.

Section Three

Project Scheduling

Developing the Project Schedule: General Guidelines

Brief History of Scheduling Techniques[1]

When Imhotep built the pyramid for pharaoh Zoser, he undoubtedly had to work out some kind of plan. He had to do the work in a certain sequence, and deciding on the sequencing of work is a part of scheduling. However, as was pointed out in Chapter Four, we do not know whether Imhotep was able to estimate with any degree of certainty how long it would take to complete each activity.

> We can't leave the haphazard to chance!
> —N.F. Simpson

No doubt he had built other structures and had some idea how long it took to quarry stone and transport it to the building site. He also should have known how many people were required to move a block of stone over a given distance. It is probable that he was able to calculate the volume of stone required for the pyramid, and thus estimate the total effort involved.

Even so, he had problems to solve that were unique, and modern scholars still argue about exactly how the huge blocks were placed as precisely as they were. Whether Imhotep was able to work out the sequence of steps required to build the pyramid using some sort of scheduling notation we don't know. But it is inconceivable to think that he built such a huge structure with no thought as to sequencing, and so we can assume that these early engineers must have developed some method of scheduling their projects.

In the 20th century, Henry Gantt developed a detailed system of scheduling using bar charts, which were subsequently called "Gantt Charts." His system, which included notation for reporting progress, has been widely used. As Figure 5.1 shows, bar charts are very easy to construct and easy to read, with one exception. By looking at the chart, it is impossible to tell whether tasks B and C are dependent on the completion of task A, or if it is just coincidence that they are planned to start at the exact time when A ends. Unless this information is available, it is difficult to determine the impact on a project if some activity gets behind ("slips," in the common terminology).

In other words, the bar chart does not show the *interrelationships* between the various tasks being done. It was this problem that led to a search for better methods in the late 1950s. One group working on this problem was the Navy, in conjunction with the consulting group of Booze, Allen, and Hamilton. They developed the PERT (**P**erformance **E**valuation and **R**eview **T**echnique) scheduling system, which was applied to the Polaris project.

Figure 5.1

Sample Bar Chart

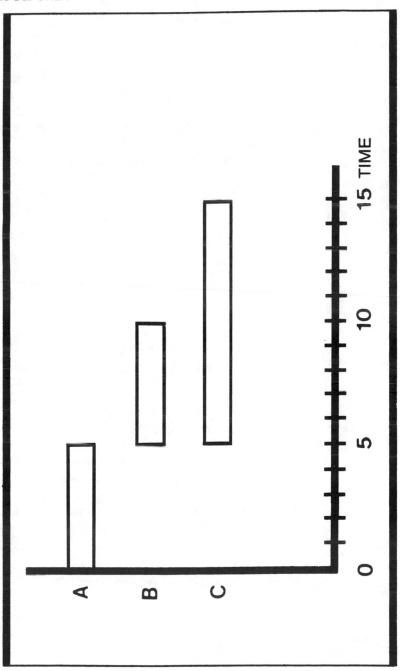

```
P — performance
E — evaluation
R — review
T — technique
```

About the same time, E.I. du Pont de Nemours Company was trying to solve the same problem and they developed CPM (Critical Path Method). The CPM system is very similar to PERT, in that activity relationships are shown by diagrams using arrows to show sequencing of work. The major difference between PERT and CPM is that PERT makes use of probabilistic methods from statistics, whereas CPM does not.

```
C — critical
P — path
M — method
```

This is a significant difference, and will be discussed in more detail in Chapter Seven. Suffice it to say that when people use nomenclature like "PERT/CPM system," suggesting that the two systems are the same, they are using improper terminology. The majority of software on the market as of this writing is CPM only. It does not permit probability analysis of networks as does PERT.

Both PERT and CPM offer a way of finding the longest path through a project. Naturally, if all activities on the longest path are not completed as scheduled (or if time lost on one activity cannot be regained on another), then the end date begins to slip accordingly. This path, therefore, is called the *critical* path—hence, the *critical path method.*

> The *critical path* in a project is the longest path, and determines the earliest date at which the work can be completed.

Network Techniques in Project Management

The first step in using the critical path method is to list all activities of the project and the graphical representation of these activities in a flow chart. This initial planning phase requires a complete analysis of the project, resources, manpower required and sequence of activities.

The starting point in scheduling should typically be the WBS, as described in Chapter Four. Beginning with the WBS allows you to develop estimates of activity durations, make personnel assignments, and so on.

Level of Detail in Scheduling

One issue involved in using the WBS and scheduling methods in combination is the level of detail to be scheduled. Even though a WBS may be developed down to level six (level-of-effort) for estimating purposes, you may want to develop a schedule for publication at level five (work package level), rather than level six.

There are two reasons for this. One is that most managers above you do not need or care about fine detail in tracking progress on a project. They only want to know where you stand on significant portions of the work. Second, you will probably find that you cannot manage well at too great a level of detail. Therefore, it may be advisable to develop a schedule to level six only for one's personal use and to publish the working schedule at level five.

> Don't plan in more detail than you can manage!

In deciding how much detail to put into a schedule, the basic rule-of-thumb is that the network should be planned in no more detail than can be managed. However, there is a converse rule, which is that planning in too little detail leads to problems as well. For example, when a number of activities are lumped together and scheduled as one task, it is difficult to determine progress, and the final activity in the sequence is likely to be crunched because preceding activities took longer than anticipated.

A related aspect of this has to do with activity duration. Tasks should be broken down into units of work which have relatively short durations. There is no hard-and-fast rule, but suggested durations should be in the range of ten to thirty days maximum, just depending on the nature of the work. If this is not done, there is a real tendency to *back-end-load* tasks, as was alluded to in the preceding paragraph. People are inclined to look at long-duration tasks at the beginning and say, "I don't need to start now—I have plenty of time."

In short, there must be a balance or compromise between scheduling in too much or too little detail. As will be shown in later chapters, breaking large tasks down into manageable ones not only keeps them from being back-end-loaded, but also helps with resource allocation. In addition, it is often possible to establish measurable milestones at which *deliverables* will be produced, thus giving a tangible measure of progress on the project.

Definitions of Network Terms

Activity

An activity (task) is any portion of the project that requires time (and possibly resources); it has a measured beginning and ending. Activities can include paperwork, labor, negotiations, machinery operations, and purchased-part lead-times. When an activity represents purchased-part lead-times or license waiting periods, it is inserted into the schedule to reflect that subsequent work can only be done after that lead-time has passed.

Using WBS terminology, an activity could be a *subtask, work package* or a *level-of-effort*. It all depends on the level of detail desired in scheduling.

Dummy Activity

An arrow which denotes nothing but a dependency of one activity upon another is a dummy activity, and carries a zero duration. Dummies are usually represented by dashed-line arrows.

Events

Beginning and ending points of activities are known as events. An event is a specific point in time. Events are commonly denoted graphically by a numbered circle.

Drawing Network Diagrams— Graphics

Several different graphical schemes exist for drawing networks. Because all schedules of any significance are, for practical reasons, almost required to be done using computers, the choice of scheduling software will likely determine which graphical scheme you will use.

Activity-on-Node Diagrams

All network diagrams make use of arrows to show the inter-relationships of work. There are two conventional forms of these. One is called the *activity-on-arrow* system. The other is *activity-on-node*. The activity-on-node network uses circles or boxes to represent activities, while the arrows which connect them only show the sequence in which work must flow. Events are usually not shown on the activity-on-node diagram. In Figure 5.2, Activity A precedes B, while the two of them are in parallel with C. Based on the diagram, Activities A, B, and C must be completed before Activity D can begin.

Activity-on-Arrow Diagrams

Figure 5.3 shows a diagram using activity-on-arrow notation. Note that this is the same network illustrated in Figure 5.2 by activity-on-node notation.

In the activity-on-arrow network, the arrow represents an activity and the circle represents an event. In the Figure 5.3 diagram, Activity A must be completed before B can begin, but A and B can be done in parallel with Activity C. Again, as was shown for the activity-on-node network, Activities A, B, and C must be completed before D can begin.

For the activity-on-arrow network, the arrow corresponds to a unit of work from the WBS. That unit may be a level-of-effort, a work package, or a subtask.

Unlike the activity-on-node network, the activity-on-arrow diagram shows distinct events. As was mentioned above, an event takes place at a point in time.

Figure 5.2

Activity-On-Node
Network

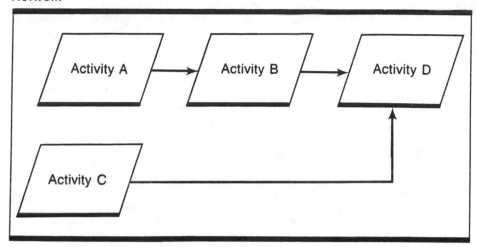

Figure 5.3

Activity-On-Arrow

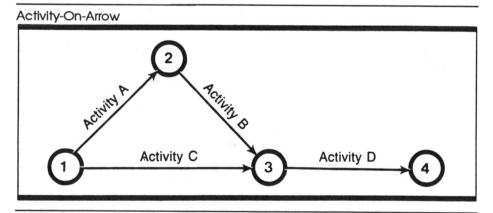

Work is completed—that is an event. That same event
might also be the point at which subsequent work can
begin. Activities can be partially completed, whereas
events can only be *achieved*.

One advantage of activity-on-arrow networks is that the events can be numbered, as shown, and the activities can be referred to in terms of their event numbers. Thus, Activity 1-2 is Activity A. This notation is called I-J notation, from mathematics. It makes data input to a computer somewhat easier than is true of activity-on-node networks, since the computer automatically knows how to link the activities by using the event numbers. With activity-on-node networks, you usually have to tell the computer exactly how everything is linked.

Common Pitfalls to Avoid

Networks are created based on logical or technical dependencies among activities. In other words, the activity "approve diagrams" must be preceded by "prepare diagrams." Generally speaking, there is no single way to draw a network. However, if the diagram shows work being done out-of-order, such as approving diagrams being done before they were prepared, then it is incorrect. This is the only way in which a network can be said to be right or wrong.

A first draft of a network may result in connecting activities in series which could be done in parallel. For example, suppose you are planning a family yardwork project. You want to mow the grass, trim the weeds around trees, trim some hedges, fertilize the lawn and clean up the trimmings. If you drew a diagram with all of these in series, you might have the result shown in Figure 5.4.

Naturally, this schedule would take less time to complete if some of the work could be done in parallel. An alternative is shown in Figure 5.5.

Another pitfall in dealing with network logic occurs when an activity is seen as totally discrete. Suppose Activity D in Figure 5.6 depends on Activities B and C being finished before it can be completed, but it depends only on having *half* of Activity A completed. In this case, the network in the first figure gives a misleading result. The correct relationship is shown by the second half of the figure, which connects the midpoint of Activity A with the node between B-C-D. If the critical path

Figure 5.4

Lawn Project with All
Activities in Series

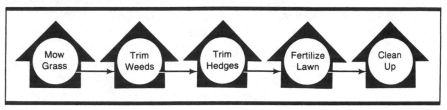

Figure 5.5

Lawn Project with
Parallel Activities

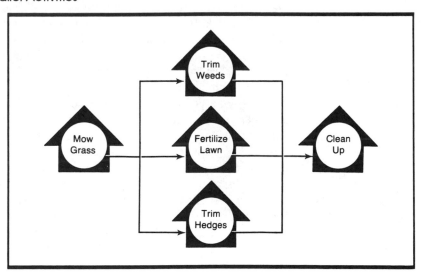

runs through the common node and Activity D, then
splitting Activity A will shorten the critical path by one-
half the duration of A.

Figure 5.6

Partial Dependency
Network

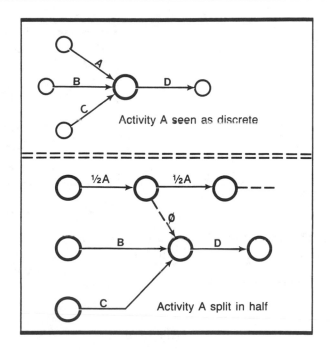

Activity A seen as discrete

Activity A split in half

A problem also occurs when a *loop* is formed in the logic, as shown in Figure 5.7. These loops defy analysis and must be avoided. Most current microcomputer software performs a loop test before doing an analysis, and will exit if a loop is found. However, if the software does not tell where the loop exists, it can be very difficult to locate.

To avoid these pitfalls, it is recommended that networks be drawn on paper before entering data into the computer. This way you can work out all logic details and check off activities as you enter them, thus helping to ensure that nothing is omitted or connected incorrectly.

Figure 5.7

Loop In Network Diagram

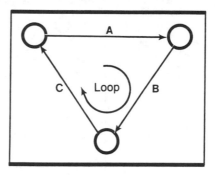

Natural and Resource Dependencies

Natural dependencies are those which occur simply because one thing cannot be done until another has been completed. You cannot deliver newspapers until they have been printed.

Resource dependencies occur because of resource limitations. One person cannot do two full-time jobs simultaneously.

Schedules should be initially developed based *only* on natural dependencies. Once a resource analysis is conducted, you may find that revisions to the schedule are required. Nevertheless, to develop a sequence based on the idea that "B cannot start until Henry becomes available" can be severely limiting. You may choose to use Charlie, rather than Henry, thus alleviating the problem.

Fixed-Time Activities

Some activities require fixed time periods outside the control of management. Examples: legal minimums (thirty to ninety days advance notice for public hearings), technical minimums, such as curing time for concrete, etc.

When these become part of the critical path, it is useful to try and accomplish in parallel other activities which can be done meanwhile. However, when possible, it is advisable to keep fixed-time activities off the critical path, since nothing can be done to shorten them in the event the end date must be advanced.

Accounting for the Weather

When it is possible for weather to cause delays in completing project work, such delays must be factored into the schedule. One method is to estimate how long a project will take, then add to that duration a fudge-factor based on considering in what part of the year the project will be underway.

A better method is to consider each activity individually and see what impact weather might have on that activity specifically, then add fudge-factors to only those activities. By doing so, you avoid padding the entire project because of a small number of activities.

It may also be possible to schedule activities that have large amounts of float during those periods when weather is likely to cause delays.

Conventional Assumptions

In scheduling projects, the following three assumptions are commonly made. As is true of all assumptions, these are often the cause of problems.

1. The time estimate made for an activity is the mean or average time which it should take, and the estimate is called the *activity duration*. Estimates of activity duration do not include uncontrollable contingencies such as fires, strikes, or legal delays.
2. In estimating activity duration, the activity should be considered independently of those that precede or follow it. For example, if an activity depends on the delivery of some materials, the delivery should be shown as an activity with its own duration. It should not be said that the second activity will probably be late because delivery of materials may not occur on schedule.
3. It is also usually assumed that a normal level of manpower, equipment and other resources will be available for each activity. Except for known limitations of resources that cause some activities to be resource-dependent, do not try to account for conflicts that may occur because activities are run in

parallel. These conflicts will be dealt with after the initial scheduling computations have been made.

Precedence Diagramming

Precedence diagramming was actually the "father" of the basic activity-on-node method. It allows the analysis of special logic relations in networks by adding "lead" and/or "lag" values to show that one activity must lead or lag behind another activity. There are at least two conventional ways of drawing precedence networks, but only one is shown in the following figures.

The start of B must lag five days after the finish of A. An example of this might be that something has been painted (Activity A) and it cannot be polished (Activity B) until the paint has thoroughly dried, the drying time being five days. (See Figure 5.8.)

The start of B must lag three days after the start of A. In this case, Activity A begins and three days later B can be started, thus possibly overlapping with A. An example might be that a person starts wiring a wall in a building (Activity A) and then another person starts sheetrock installation (Activity B) three days later, while wiring of the building continues. (See Figure 5.9.)

The finish of B must lag four days after the finish of A. The sheetrock mentioned in the preceding paragraph will be finished a little behind the completion of all wiring. (See Figure 5.10.)

The finish of B must lag thirty-five days after the start of A. (See Figure 5.11.)

The start of B must lag four days after the start of A and the finish of B must lag four days after the finish of A. This is the conventional ladder or lead-lag network, which is discussed in the following section of this chapter. (See Figure 5.12.)

Overlapping Work—Ladder Networks

While precedence networks offer a simplified way of portraying the overlapping of work, it is possible to show such activities using conventional arrow diagrams.

In many cases, both the start and finish dates for a project have been "given" before the project manager begins planning the work. The end date may be dictated

Figure 5.8

Finish-to-Start Network

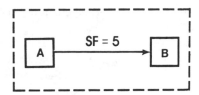

Figure 5.9

Start-to-Start Network

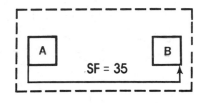

Figure 5.10

Finish-to-Finish Network

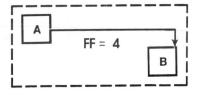

Figure 5.11

Start-to-Finish Network

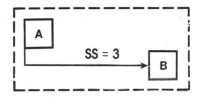

Figure 5.12

A Composite
Start-to-Start and
Finish-to-Finish Network

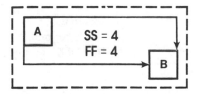

by market or customer requirements, whereas the start date is constrained because one project is already in progress and must be completed before the new one can begin.

Given this fairly typical scenario, the network is developed, the critical path is computed and the total project duration won't "fit" between the two given dates. The critical path is too long, and must be shortened. (It is the old problem of trying to fit ten pounds of trash into a five-pound bag.)

It may be possible to shorten the critical path by putting more people on the task(s), although all work has a point at which adding resources does not shorten the job, and may, in fact, actually increase the time required because people get in each other's way. (Or the two may argue about how to do the job, thus wasting time.)

An earlier example showed that it may not be necessary to completely finish one task before beginning another. The technique is to overlap the work. Consider the following example. Suppose you want to dig a ditch in which some pipe will be laid. Once the pipe is laid, you will cover the trench.

Now you might be inclined to simply tie the pipe-laying task on the end of digging, followed by covering, so you would have a sequential network.

This will clearly create the longest path to complete the project. The question is, do you need to dig the whole trench before you begin laying pipe? And do you need to lay all of the pipe before you begin covering?

The answer is "no," but you must get a certain amount of trench dug before you can start laying pipe, and similarly, you must lay a certain amount of pipe before you start covering. The delay before the subsequent activity can start is called "lead" time. Diagramming this set of activities, you have the ladder network shown in Figure 5.13.

The x elements are called *lead* elements and the y elements are called *lag* elements. We now have a path from beginning to end which is shorter than that obtained by simply connecting the three activities in series.

Figure 5.13

Ladder Network
for a Pipeline

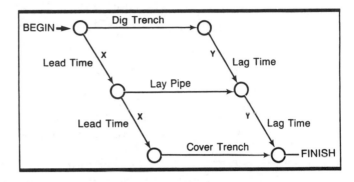

This example illustrates one of the principle ways of shortening schedules when work does not have to be totally complete before a dependent task can begin. However, not all software will properly analyze ladder networks, which might be a factor to consider in deciding which software package to buy.

Key Points

- Scheduling considers both the *durations* of tasks and the *sequence* in which the work must be done.

- The bar chart is also called a *Gantt chart*.

- Bar charts do not show *interrelationships* of work, and thus do not permit an easy analysis of impact on a project if one activity slips.

- PERT uses probabilistic methods, whereas CPM does not.

- The critical path is the longest path through a project and therefore determines the earliest end date.

- Don't plan in more detail than you can manage.

- Activity-on-node notation uses the nodes to represent activities and the arrows to show the sequence in which they are performed.

- Activity-on-arrow notation uses the arrows to represent activities and the nodes to represent events.

- Precedence diagrams show special logic relationships. Conventional networks can do the same, but are more complex.

- Diagram using natural dependencies only.

- Be careful about the three conventional assumptions.

Schedule
Computations

Once a suitable network has been drawn with durations
assigned to all activities, it is necessary to perform computations to determine the longest path through the
project. If start and finish dates have already been dictated for the project, these calculations will tell whether
the required dates can be met. If only the start date is
given, the computations will tell the earliest completion
date for the project.

> The *critical path* is the longest path through a
> project, and so determines the earliest comple-
> tion for the work.

The simplest computation that can be made for a network will determine total working time on the longest path through the project and will reveal whether any latitude exists on paths parallel to the longest path. The longest path is called the critical path, since a slip on the longest path will cause a corresponding slip in the completion of the project. This computation would tell how many weeks (or days or hours, depending on time units being used) it will take to complete the project if no holidays or vacation periods exist.

Naturally, during certain parts of the year, holidays and/or vacations will intervene, so that the actual calendar time for the project is likely to exceed the working time.

It is also important to note that the conventional way to compute project working times is to ignore resources initially. In other words, activities are treated as though they have *fixed durations*, based on the assumption that certain levels of resources will be available when the work begins.

Further, these durations are estimated from historical data and are based on a person being available who has a certain skill-level to do the work. As was pointed out in previous chapters, if these conditions are not met, then the actual working times will deviate from estimated times, sometimes considerably.

Network Rules

In order to compute project working times, there are only two rules which are universal in defining how networks function. These are listed below as rules one and two. Additional rules are sometimes imposed on the network by computer software. These are strictly a function of the software and are not applied to all networks. Examples of the more common rules are listed below as rules three through six.

Rule I: Before a task can begin, all tasks preceding it must be completed.

Rule 2: Arrows denote logical precedence. Neither the length of the arrow or its angular direction have any significance. (It is not a vector, but a scalar.)

Note: Rules 3–6 apply *only* if the software programmer *says so!* They *do not* apply to all networks!

Rule 3: Event numbers cannot be duplicated in a network. This only applies to activity-on-arrow networks. This rule might be violated if a large project is broken down into subprojects, since there would be no confusion over having an Event 3 in subproject A and an Event 3 in subproject B.

Rule 4: Any two events may be directly connected by not more than one activity. This rule means that you cannot tie two activities in parallel using the same two events. Figure 6.1 contains an example of tying two activities directly in parallel, followed by an example showing how they are connected when rule four applies (Figure 6.2). Note the dummy, which indicates that the two events really take place at the same point in time.

Rule 5: Networks are allowed only one initial event (nothing preceding) and only one terminal event. There are times when it is convenient to have multiple beginning and ending events— such as when multiple-project resource allocation is being done by putting all projects into the computer as if they were one big project, so the computer can allocate resources across them. See Figure 6.3.

Rule 6: Event numbers must flow from left-to-right in ascending order. This is a particularly onerous rule, since it requires that following events be renumbered if a new activity is inserted into the network. This rule was common in the

Figure 6.1

Parallel Activities

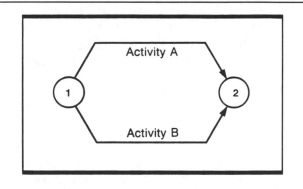

Figure 6.2

Parallel Activities Rule 4

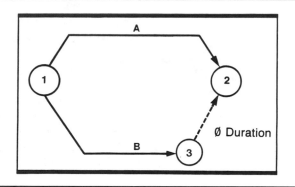

Figure 6.3

Project with Two
Beginning Events

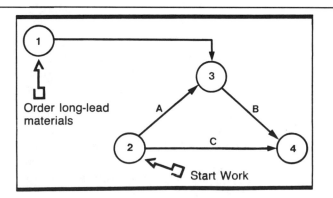

early days of computerized scheduling, but is seldom seen today.

Basic Scheduling Computations

Although no one is likely to do network computations manually in this day of abundant scheduling software, it is important to understand how computations are made by the computer. Otherwise, it is easy to fall into the "garbage-in-garbage-out" problem. Further, the computer output is not easily understandable unless the computation method is understood. For example: What does float really mean? What is the difference between total float and free float?

The following material will explain how the basic computations are performed without concern for resource limitations. That is, these computations are based on the assumption that the required resources will indeed be available when time comes to do the work. This is equivalent to saying that the organization has an unlimited pool of people, which of course is never the case. For this reason, a schedule which assumes unlimited resources is considered to be the ideal or best-case situation and provides a starting point for resource-constrained project scheduling. Chapter Seven deals with the allocation of resources to yield a realistic working schedule.

The network used to illustrate scheduling computations is in activity-on-arrow format, because I feel it is easier to show how the calculations are made in this scheme. However, the same exact results are obtained using activity-on-node format. (See Figure 6.4.)

Note that the activities are labeled with letters, and events are numbered. Thus, the event following Activity A is Event 2, etc. The numbers under the activities are working durations in days. Each event is divided in half so that the *earliest time* can be placed on the left side and the *latest time* can be placed on the right side. Other notation schemes are used in other books. This one just seems to me to be very simple to understand.

In order to locate the critical path and compute earliest and latest start and finish times for non-critical project activities, it is necessary to do two sets of computations. These are called *forward-pass* and *backward-pass* calculations. The steps in performing those calculations will be illustrated using the network in Figure 6.4.

Forward Pass Computations

A forward pass is made through the network to calculate the earliest achievement times for each event in the network. For an event at the end of an activity, the earliest event time is called the *earliest finish*. When the event is at the beginning of an activity, it is called the *earliest start* for the activity. As was stated above, the times shown on the activities in Figure 6.4 are *working days*. The project is shown as starting at time $T = 0$. Once event times are determined, they can be converted to calendar dates, but that step will be omitted in this chapter.

Rule

> When two or more activities enter a node, the earliest time when that event can be achieved is the *larger* of the durations on the paths entering the node. This is the result of Network Rule 1, which says that work following an event cannot begin until all work leading up to the event has been completed. Another way to say this is that the *longest path* will dictate the earliest date at which the event can be achieved.

Figure 6.5 shows the first steps in the forward-pass computation. Event 2 can be achieved eight days after the project starts, because Activity A has that duration and is the only path leading to Event 2.

However, there are two paths leading to Event 3, one along Activities A-C and the other across Activity B. Since Event 2 can be achieved as early as eight days into the job, continuing along Activity C would allow achievement of Event 3 on day eleven. The duration of Activity B, however, is fifteen days, so Event 3 cannot be achieved until day fifteen—the *larger* of the two numbers, which is based on the longest path to the event.

Figure 6.4

Network to Illustrate
Computation Methods

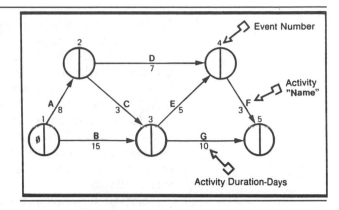

Figure 6.5

Forward Pass to
Determine Earliest Time
at Event

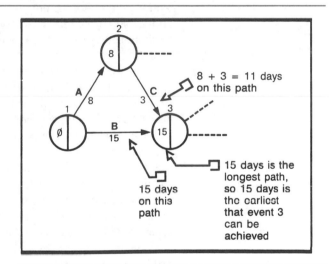

Figure 6.6

Network With Earliest
Times Shown

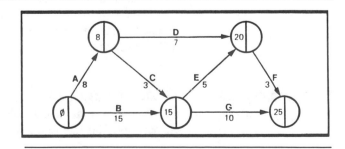

The remaining forward-pass computations are made the same way, yielding the event times shown in Figure 6.6. Note that the earliest completion for the project is twenty-five working days.

Given the activity durations shown and the sequences detailed by the network, the project has a completion date twenty-five working days after it begins. This working time can now be compared to a calendar to determine if a proposed end date can be met, given an anticipated start date. If it cannot, then either the project must start earlier, the end date must slip out or the network must be changed to compress (shorten) the critical path.

Suppose, for example, that the work must be finished on a date that corresponds to twenty-three working days after the proposed start. We know that the critical path, which has a twenty-five day duration, must be shortened by two days. Would any other path be affected?

The answer to this question is never obvious in a complicated network. In order to see what else in the network might have to change, more information is needed. Specifically, we need to know the *latest* times by which each event can be achieved and still meet the twenty-five-day end date.

You might ask, "Why not use the twenty-three-day end date, since that is what is required?" The answer is that a *best-case* computation is made first. The best case would be one in which the twenty-five-day finish is acceptable. This is considered the best case because allowing the project to extend beyond that time is not making best use of resources, given that twenty-five days is possible.

For that reason, we assign a twenty-five-day *late time* to the final event, and then do a *backward pass computation* to determine the latest event times which will permit achievement of the twenty-five-day completion.

Backward Pass Computations

As was stated above, a backward pass is made through the network to compute the *latest times* for each event in the network. This latest time will represent the *latest fin-*

ish for a preceding activity and a *latest start* for a suc-
ceeding one. This computation is made by subtracting
activity durations from previous event late times. See
Figure 6.7.

Rule

> When two or more activities leave a node, the
> latest time when that event can be achieved is
> the *smaller* of working times given by subtracting
> activity durations from previous event late times.
> In other words, the latest event time will be the
> *earliest* of the times when two or more paths
> both lead back to that event. This is illustrated in
> Figure 6.7.

Beginning at Event 5 and working backward, subtract the three-day duration of Activity F from
twenty-five and the late time for Event 4 is twenty-two.
Now subtract the five-day duration of Activity E from
twenty-two and you get seventeen days on that path.
Note, however, that path G also leads back to Event 3,
and by subtracting the ten-day duration of G from the
twenty-five-day end time on Event 5, you have fifteen.
The choice, then, is between fifteen or seventeen days,
and the rule says to take the smaller number. Therefore,

Figure 6.7

Backward Pass to
Determine Latest Times
at an Event

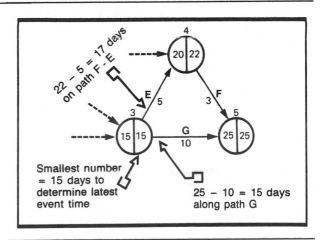

the latest time for Event 3 is fifteen days, which is the same as its earliest time. Continuing in this way, you arrive at the late event times shown in Figure 6.8.

Event Slack

Referring to Figure 6.8, note that the earliest finish for Activity A is the earliest start for Activity D. That is, $EF_A = ES_D$. Also the latest finish for A is the latest start for D. ($LF_A = LS_D$)

The difference between EF_A and LF_A is called *slack*, which gives a measure of latitude on the *event*. This slack can be used to help manage resources better, as will be discussed later. What is important to note is

Figure 6.8

Network to Illustrate
CPM Analysis

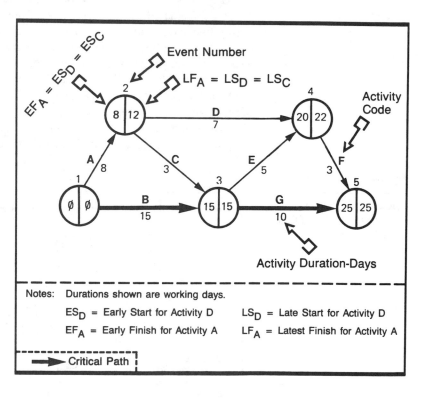

Notes: Durations shown are working days.
ES_D = Early Start for Activity D LS_D = Late Start for Activity D
EF_A = Early Finish for Activity A LF_A = Latest Finish for Activity A

➤ Critical Path

the *physical meaning* of slack. The term slack is used to indicate that the event (following Activity A, for example) can occur as early as the early time shown (eight days for Event 2) or as late as the late time shown (twelve days).

Event 2 can therefore move around from as early as day eight to as late as day twelve and the project completion time of twenty-five days can still be met. Note, however, that if Event 2 occurs any later than day twelve, the end date for the project will be impacted.

Activity Maximum Float

Now examine Activity D. Based on the beginning event, Activity D can start as early as day eight, and can also end as late as day twenty-two. The *distance* between those times is fourteen days. The activity itself takes seven days to complete. The difference between the fourteen-day distance between the two events and the seven-day working time leaves seven days in which Activity D can *float* around. This is called *maximum float* for Activity D. The equation for calculating maximum float for an activity follows (written in terms of Activity D):

$$\text{MAXIMUM FLOAT}_D = LF_D - ES_D - \text{DURATION}_D$$

It is more important to know the physical meaning of float than to try to remember the equation. If you know the physical meaning of the terms, you can always write the equations, which are quite simple.

Also, note that float and slack have different physical meanings, although practicing project managers seldom make a distinction between them. Rather, they use the terms interchangeably, as a synonym for *latitude*. However, strictly speaking, slack only applies to events and float only applies to activities. Naturally, in activity-on-node networks, which do not portray events, slack is not portrayed.

Free Float

To continue the analysis of the network, note that the latest time that Activity D can begin is day twelve and the earliest it can be completed is day twenty. The distance between those two dates is eight days. Since the activity takes seven days to complete, it can still float around for one day between those event times. This is called minimum float or *free float*. That float is more-or-less "free" to Activity D, so long as other activities that affect the early and late times for Activity D do not slip past their late times. The free float for Activity D is largely determined by the other elements of the network.

The maximum float, on the other hand, will be available only if Activity A gets completed on time and if Activity E is allowed to slip to its latest completion time of twenty-two days. The equation for free float is as follows (again, written in terms of Activity D):

$$\text{FREE FLOAT}_D = \text{EF}_D - \text{LS}_D - \text{DURATION}_D$$

The Critical Path

Now examine path B–G. There is no latitude on this path. That is, the float for Activity B is zero and the same is true for Activity G. By convention, this is called the *Critical Path*. Since this path has no float, if any of the work on the path falls behind schedule, then the end date will slip accordingly.

> An activity is a critical activity any time it has no float. Similarly, an event is a critical event when it has no slack.

Constrained End Date

It is possible that an end date has been imposed on the project (I don't believe there is any other kind of project), either by contract with the customer or by management, based on business considerations. This end date may be earlier than the earliest completion date determined by the forward pass computation, in which case the project must be started earlier or the schedule must be shortened somehow. Generally, as was mentioned previously, the start date for a project is often dictated by availability of resources or some other factor, so that the start date cannot be moved up. When this is true, then the critical path must be shortened. However, other paths may be problems as well.

For the network just analyzed, suppose the end date was established as twenty-three days after project start. What would be the overall impact on the project? To answer that question, a new backward-pass calculation must be made. Note that there is no need to do a new forward-pass computation, since the forward-pass only determines early times, and these will not change until an activity duration is changed or else the network is redrawn.

Figure 6.9 shows the network with the latest project completion constrained to twenty-three days. Now path E-F has zero float, so it is a critical path, while path B-G has -2 days of float. That is, path B-G has *negative* float, and so is called *supercritical*. In addition, the beginning event has negative slack of two days, indicating that the project needs to start two days earlier in order to meet the imposed end time. Also, the intermediate event between Activities B and G has -2 days of slack, similarly indicating a problem.

What is interesting about this network is that if Activity G is shortened by two days, the end date can be met, but there are now two critical paths. One is Activity G, while the other consists of Activities E and F. (See Figure 6.10.) Does it matter?

The answer to the question above is "yes." If float is considered to be an indicator of risk, then those activities with large amounts of float are less risky than those which have very little. An activity with float has some latitude should unforeseen problems occur with the work or if the estimate of activity duration turns out to have been low. Clearly, an activity with no float is riskier than one which has float.

For this reason, if two critical paths exist, the total project risk has been increased. To reduce that risk, an attempt should be made to get rid of all but one critical path. This can only be done by changing the duration of one or more activities, by allowing the end date to be extended, or by redrawing the network to have a new configuration. Assuming that a choice must be made of which critical path to eliminate, the issue is how to decide which path would be best to get off the critical path.

Figure 6.9

Project with Imposed
End Date Earlier Than
Earliest Finish

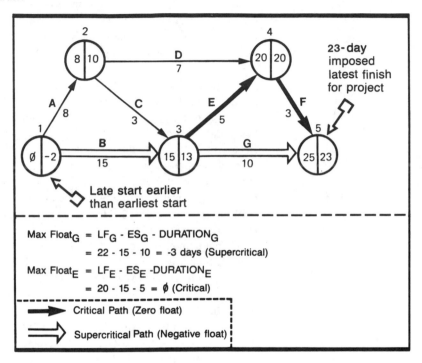

23- day
imposed
latest finish
for project

Late start earlier
than earliest start

Max Float$_G$ = LF$_G$ - ES$_G$ - DURATION$_G$

= 22 - 15 - 10 = -3 days (Supercritical)

Max Float$_E$ = LF$_E$ - ES$_E$ -DURATION$_E$

= 20 - 15 - 5 = $\emptyset$ (Critical)

→ Critical Path (Zero float)

⟹ Supercritical Path (Negative float)

Figure 6.10

Network with Dual
Critical Paths

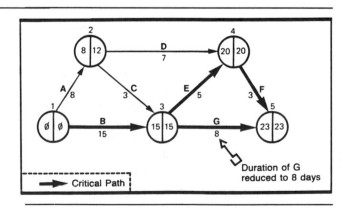

Duration of G
reduced to 8 days

→ Critical Path

There is no single answer to this problem. Float is only one kind of risk involved in a project. There are also risks from technical problems, poor estimates, weather and other uncontrollable factors. Table 6.1 contains a list of factors which should be considered in making a decision. The comments following each factor explain the rationale for appropriate decision making.

Since dual critical paths are unacceptable, it would be better to shorten Activity B to thirteen days and leave Activity G alone. As is shown in Figure 6.11, doing this allows the twenty-three day end date to be met and leaves float on all paths except B–G.

Whether a path can be shortened depends on three factors: Can the work be done faster by increasing efficiency (perhaps by using that more productive person mentioned previously)? Can the scope of the work be reduced? Can extra people be put on the job to get it done faster? It is not always possible to reduce schedule time by adding more resources since a point of *diminishing returns* is reached, often because people simply get in each other's way.

The only other possibility for meeting an earlier date would be to somehow redraw the network, perhaps using a ladder network or other method of overlapping work. What should *not* be done is to sacrifice the quality of the work by leaving time and scope unchanged and simply "throwing it together."

Figure 6.11

Activity B Shortened to Achieve 23-Day Completion

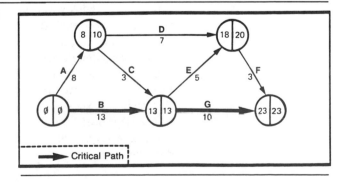

117

Table 6.1

Factors to Consider in Eliminating a Dual Critical Path	Number of activities	Path with most activities might be most risky.
	Skill level of people	Path with least-skilled people could be most risky.
	Technical risk	Path with greatest technical risk should have float.
	Weather/ uncontrollable	Give float to activities with uncontrollable factors.
	Cost	Give float to activities which cost most to do.
	Historical data	Least historical data—give float; Historically a problem—ditto.
	Available backup plan	Give float to activities with no obvious backup.
	Business cycle	If business tends to get hectic at certain times, give float to activities affected.
	Difficulty	Float given to activities which are most difficult.

Converting Arrow Diagrams to Bar Charts

While an arrow diagram is essential to do a proper analysis of the relationships between the activities in a project, and in order to find the longest path through the project, the best *working tool* is the bar chart. Those people doing the work will find it much easier to see when they are supposed to start and finish their jobs with a bar chart. The schedule shown as an arrow diagram in Figure 6.8 has been portrayed as a bar chart in Figure 6.12, making use of what was learned about the schedule from the network analysis.

In Figure 6.12, the critical path activities are shown as solid bars, while those that have float are shown as hollow bars with dots trailing to indicate the amount of float. Note that *maximum float* is shown. Also note that each activity is shown starting at its earliest possible time, so that float is reserved to be used only if absolutely necessary. This is the conventional method of displaying bar charts.

Figure 6.12

Bar Chart for Network
in Figure 6.8

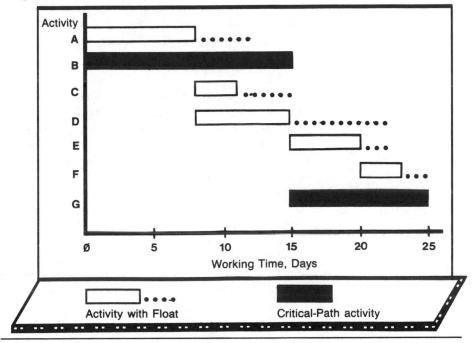

Note that Activity A is shown having four days of float and the same is true of Activity C. Initially, before the project begins, there are four days of float available for each activity. However, if Activity A slips to its latest finish of twelve weeks, then there is no float left for Activity C, and it would therefore be critical.

This illustrates a real pitfall of bar charts. Assume that different individuals are doing Activities A and C. Since the chart does not show interrelationships of activities, it would be hard for those performing the work to tell that the float is shared between Activities A and C. They would look at the chart and each would think there were four days of float. Naturally, if each tried to take that float, the project is in trouble.

| Parkinson's Law | Work always expands to take the time allowed. |

| Lewis' Law for Float | If you give it to them, they'll take it! |

In fact, Parkinson's law can be applied to project float. Parkinson's law says that work always expands to fit the time allowed. When applied to float, it means that when you give them float, they take it! For this reason, some software does not print float. The implication of such a schedule is simply that the work should be done as shown.

Indeed, it is always a good idea to keep float in reserve to be used if an estimate turns out to be wrong or if an unforeseen problem causes the work to be delayed. As someone told me recently, every project should be planned as if there will be at least some percentage of the total time when the entire city will have a power blackout and nothing will get done.

Limitations of Critical Path Method

It is important to remember what was pointed out earlier—namely that the conventional critical path analysis, which has been illustrated for this network, assumes that unlimited resources exist in the organization, so all activities can be done as planned. As the bar chart shows, however, a number of points exist at which activities are running in parallel. If those activities require the same resources, then there may not be enough to get the job done as shown, so the schedule cannot be met. This subject is addressed in Chapter Seven.

Multiple Calendars

One final subject must be considered in doing basic network computations. Not all project activities can follow the same working schedule. Does everyone work Monday through Friday? Do some people only work weekends?

In some projects there may be activities that require actual working days to complete, while others do not. Pouring of concrete must be done during the work week. However, that concrete may cure over a weekend. For this reason, it is important that multiple calendars be considered in scheduling.

Consider, for example, the situation in which one group works a conventional Monday-Friday schedule. Another group, however, only works weekends—Saturday and Sunday. This is shown in Figure 6.13.

Suppose the two groups are scheduled to do two sequential tasks, with Group 1 working exactly one week (M-F), followed by the people in Group 2, who are supposed to finish their work over the weekend. However, Group 1 gets behind on their work by one day. How much is the schedule impacted? As Figure 6.14 shows, the work will slip an entire week because Group 1 gets behind only one day!

This kind of problem highlights the need for multiple calendars in scheduling. They are called calendars, since holiday and overtime dates are different for the two groups. If the software being used does not permit the use of multiple calendars, it may still be possible to "fake it" and force the schedule to reflect correct working dates, but it may be difficult to do. For this reason, selection of software should be made with this potential requirement in mind.

Figure 6.13

Multiple Calendar
Network

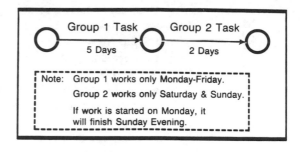

Figure 6.14

Work Slips One Week
Because of a One-Day
Slip by Group 1

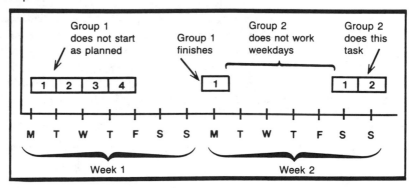

Key Points

_____

- Scheduling is done to work out sequencing of work and to show earliest completion for a project and points at which latitude exists in the work.

- Only two rules govern *all* networks. The others are a function of the software being used.

- The *forward-pass* computation determines earliest finish times for activities. The *backward-pass* calculation determines latest finish times.

- Critical path computations assume unlimited resources, and thus may not be achievable.

- Slack strictly applies only to events, and float only applies to activities. In practice, the terms are used interchangeably.

- Try to get rid of all but one critical path in a network, since critical activities increase risk.

CHAPTER 7 Resource Constraints

Chapter One stated that the key to project scheduling is to solve the resource allocation problem. Every organization has a fixed number of resources. Yet project managers invariably plan their projects as if each individual's project were the only one being done! Then when they get ready to do a particular task, they find that "Charlie" is already tied up on another job. Then the screaming starts.

"I can't get my job done on time if you don't break Charlie loose from the job he's working on," the frustrated manager bellows.

"We need Charlie on this job. The product is being shipped to upper Mongolia next Friday, and this is our big chance to penetrate that market. This job has priority over yours."

"Well, give me someone else."

"Sorry. There is no one else available. You'll just have to do the best you can until we get through with the Mongolian project."

If that weren't bad enough, when Charlie is finally free to work on the lower priority project (which by now has become the top-priority job because it is running late), the manager discovers that he has Charlie scheduled to work on two activities at the same time, and they are both full-time jobs! He hadn't noticed that the two activities were running in parallel. Now what does he do? Should Charlie work eighty-hour weeks until the jobs are complete?

This illustrates the problem with the basic PERT/CPM procedures used to produce project schedules. They are limited because resource availabilities and requirements are not included in the scheduling process. The computation procedure assumes that resource availability is unlimited and that, given the durations assigned to activities, only precedence requirements affect start/completion times. For this reason, PERT and CPM have been criticized as a *feasible way to produce a non-feasible result!*

Fortunately, there is help available today! Numerous software programs exist to run on personal computers, which will schedule work to be done in such a way that the most efficient use is made of resources. This chapter illustrates the use of one such program, Project Workbench™, produced by Applied Business -Technologies.

This program was used because it represents a fair tradeoff among all of the characteristics of a good scheduling program. It is doubtful that any package will have all of the characteristics that you may want, so ultimately you have to pick the one with the best overall features and use it. As of this writing, there are around 150 programs available to run on personal computers, and no one has time or resources to evaluate all of them.

The Effect of Limited Resources on Schedule Float[1]

When network computations are made, float is calculated based on activity interrelationships and durations. When resource limitations exist, the float that appeared to be available under straightforward critical-path analysis may not exist. When resources are limited, float can be affected as follows:

- Resource constraints reduce the total amount of schedule float.
- Scheduling times are not unique; float values are not unique. When a resource is overloaded, such conflicts are solved by applying certain scheduling rules which are called *heuristics*. The term means "rule-of-thumb," and will be discussed later in this chapter.
- The critical path in a resource-constrained schedule may not be the identical continuous series of activities obtained in the unlimited resources schedule. A continuous chain of zero-float tasks may exist, but since task start times are constrained by resource availability and precedence relations, this chain may include different activities.

To illustrate the resource allocation problem, the network developed in Chapter Six will be used, and resources will be assigned to each activity. How resources are assigned to activities depends on the nature of the work involved and the people available to do the work.

In some cases, work can be done by anyone available. Many kinds of manual labor fit into this category. For example, sweeping floors, mowing grass and other forms of housework might be done by any available person at least ten years of age or older. When this is the case, those individuals available to do work are treated as a resource *pool*.

As another example, if a group of skilled carpenters were available, it might be possible for any of them to install a new door in a room. However, all carpenters are not necessarily equal. Some may not be able to do certain jobs, so treating them as a "pool" of resources would not work.

When workers can all do a given job, it is useful to consider how task duration varies with resource level. In Figure 7.1 is an illustration of the relationship. If five workers can do a task in twenty days, we say that 100 man-days[2] of labor will be expended. This combination of labor and task duration can be portrayed as a rectangle, and the area of the rectangle represents the units "man-days."

If it is assumed that equal-area rectangles will yield the same result so far as work is concerned, then adding labor to the task will shorten the task duration. For the example given, adding five workers would allow completion of the work in ten days. Putting twenty workers on the job would allow it to be completed in five days, or half the original time.

Naturally, this cannot be extended so far. For all work there must be a point at which adding workers does not shorten the job. Instead, the people will begin to get in each other's way, and the time taken to do the job will begin to increase, rather than decrease. For this

Figure 7.1

Equal-Area Labor
Rectangles

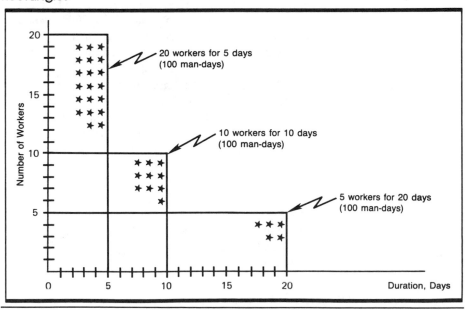

128

reason, a project manager might choose to treat an activity duration as *fixed*, and assign only so many workers to it.

On the other hand, if the activity is such that duration can be changed by applying variable levels of resources, then there would be no exact duration for the task assigned to the project. Rather, the project manager might treat the initial duration and resource level as only a starting point and allow the actual task duration to vary in order to achieve a certain desired schedule. It might be that a prescribed end date must be met, and it is feasible to add as many resources as required to meet that deadline. Or it might be that what is desired is to finish the project in the shortest time, given a certain number of people available to do the work.

The most common scheduling method is to assume fixed-duration tasks, so that system will be illustrated first, followed by scheduling the same project using variable-duration tasks.

Scheduling With Fixed-Duration Activities

In most projects, the starting point would be to assume that a certain number of people will be assigned to an activity, and that it will then require so many days (or whatever time units are appropriate) to complete. Figure 7.2 repeats the schedule from Chapter Six, with task durations and resource levels shown. We will begin by analyzing the situation in which a pool of workers is available, all of whom can do any of the activities in the project. Again, the analysis which follows was done using Project Workbench, Version 3.1.

Before the computer can do a resource allocation, the number of workers available must be specified. For this project, two categories of workers were specified:

Description	Number Available	Man-Days/ Week
Senior Worker	2	10
Helper	1	5

Two Senior Workers are available. If a normal five-day work week is assumed, then there are ten man-days of labor available to apply to the project each week. For the Helpers, one is available, yielding five man-days of labor each week.

Note that holidays and vacations serve to reduce the amount of labor available during the period in which they occur, so that the schedule will reflect a total elapsed time greater than would be obtained if a constant level of labor were available. Project Workbench allows the levels of available resources to be varied upward and downward from the average level to compensate for availability of overtime or holidays. This means that vacation days can be entered for individuals when resources are tracked on an individual

Figure 7.2

Network to Illustrate
CPM Analysis

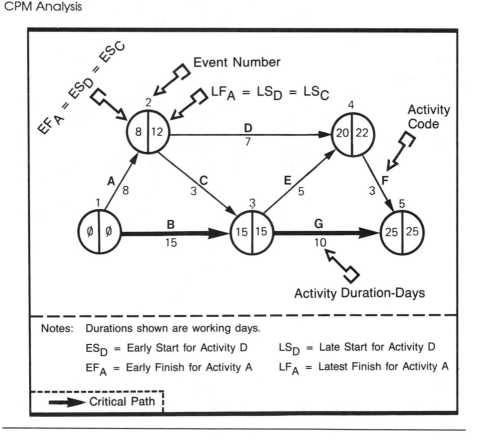

Notes: Durations shown are working days.

ES_D = Early Start for Activity D   LS_D = Late Start for Activity D

EF_A = Early Finish for Activity A   LF_A = Latest Finish for Activity A

Critical Path

basis, and the schedule will be adjusted to compensate for those days.

For the analysis which follows, no vacations have been entered, but standard legal holidays are left in the program to show the effect of having days on which no one works.

As each activity is entered into the computer, a level of resources is assigned to each task. The levels assigned are shown in Table 7.1.

Once the data has been input to the computer, a critical path analysis can be done. The first analysis is made as described in Chapter Six, assuming that unlimited resources are available. This schedule is shown in Figure 7.3. Using June 17, 1991 as a starting date, the project will end on July 23, 1991. This corresponds to twenty-five working days, as was calculated for the arrow diagram previously. However, because July 4 is a holiday, it is dropped from working time, so that the actual end date is twenty-six days from project start.

Also note that an activity called "Finish" has been entered into the project. This is done to force Project Workbench to show exactly when the project ends, but the software will not accept a zero duration activity, so it automatically assigns a one-day duration to Finish. This means the project really would end on July 22.

Note that at the bottom of the schedule the computer shows the level of each resource required to do the work as scheduled. These levels are shown in man-days required each week. Since the July 4th week is a four-

Table 7.1

Resources Allocated to
Project

Activity	Duration	Senior Worker	Helper
A	8	8	0
B	15	15	3
C	3	0	3
D	7	7	2
E	5	5	0
F	3	3	1
G	10	20	10

Notes: Durations in days
Allocations in man-days total

Figure 7.3

Bar Chart for Network
in Figure 7.2

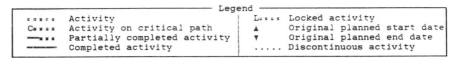

```
┌──────────────────────── Project description ────────────────────────┐
│  Report: Gantt Chart          Date:   1-07-91          Time: 10:20  │
│                                                                      │
│  Title: Project Zero          Project ID: SP           Version: 1  │
│                                                                      │
│  Manager: Jim Lewis           Project filename: ZERO6  Dept:       │
│                                                                      │
│  Project start:  6-17-91      Project end:             Budget:     │
│                                                                      │
│  Description:  Small Network to illustrate resource scheduling     │
└──────────────────────────────────────────────────────────────────────┘
```

```
┌──────────────────────────── Legend ────────────────────────────┐
│  ▪▪▪▪▪  Activity                    L▪▪▪▪ Locked activity        │
│  C▪▪▪▪  Activity on critical path    ▲    Original planned start date │
│  ▬▪▪▪   Partially completed activity ▼    Original planned end date   │
│  ▬▬▬▬   Completed activity          ..... Discontinuous activity │
└──────────────────────────────────────────────────────────────────┘
```

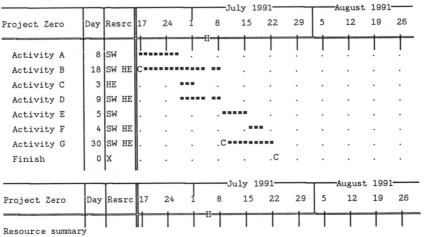

```
                                    ─July 1991─      ─August 1991─
Project Zero   Day Resrc  17   24   1   8   15  22  29   5   12  19  26

Activity A      8 |SW    ▪▪▪▪▪▪▪▪  .   .   .   .   .   .   .   .   .
Activity B     18 |SW HE C▪▪▪▪▪▪▪▪▪▪▪▪ ▪▪  .   .   .   .   .   .   .
Activity C      3 |HE    |.      .  ▪▪▪  .   .   .   .   .   .   .   .
Activity D      9 |SW HE |.      .  ▪▪▪▪▪ ▪▪ .   .   .   .   .   .   .
Activity E      5 |SW    |.      .   .  ▪▪▪▪▪▪ .   .   .   .   .   .
Activity F      4 |SW HE |.      .   .   . ▪▪▪ .   .   .   .   .   .
Activity G     30 |SW HE |.      .   .  .C▪▪▪▪▪▪▪▪▪▪ .   .   .   .   .
Finish          0 |X     |.      .   .   .   .C .   .   .   .   .
```

```
                                    ─July 1991─      ─August 1991─
Project Zero   Day Resrc  17   24   1   8   15  22  29   5   12  19  26
```

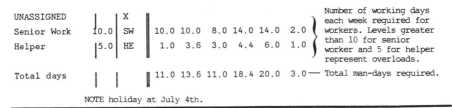

Resource summary

Utilization

```
                                                     Number of working days
UNASSIGNED      |   |  X                              each week required for
Senior Work  |10.0| SW    10.0 10.0  8.0 14.0 14.0  2.0 ⎫ workers. Levels greater
Helper        |5.0| HE     1.0  3.6  3.0  4.4  6.0  1.0 ⎬ than 10 for senior
                                                         ⎭ worker and 5 for helper
                                                           represent overloads.
Total days    |   |   |  11.0 13.6 11.0 18.4 20.0  3.0 — Total man-days required.
```

NOTE holiday at July 4th.

day week, the levels drops that week.

On the left of the resource listing is the level of resources available in man-days per week. As long as the level required is less than the level available, the schedule can be met as shown under ideal conditions. This is not the case, however. There are points at which the required level of Senior Workers is greater than ten, meaning that they are overloaded, and the same is true for the Helper. To see the impact of this resource shortage on the schedule, a new analysis is done.

For Project Workbench, this analysis is called *Autoschedule*, with resources being considered. Figure 7.4 shows the result. The completion of the project slips to August 7, 1991. Note that the software schedules Activity G to be done before it does Activities E and F. It gives priority to critical path activities, delaying non-critical-path work until more resources become available. In this case, sufficient resources did not become available until Activity G was completed, so the computer scheduled E and F to be done then.

This illustrates what happens to many projects when sufficient resources are not available to do the work as planned. Without a good scheduling tool, the project manager often is not aware that the project is resource-limited until the work begins. Then it is too late.

To compensate, overtime may be applied to the project—in essence increasing resource availability. This may not solve the problem, however, since more labor may be needed than can be gained with overtime. In the case of this network, the Senior Workers were scheduled to work fourteen man days per week during the latter part of the project, which would be about equivalent to working six days per week for each individual. That might not be too bad, if it were only for a short period.

However, studies have shown that results gained with overtime tend to be short-lived. After several weeks of working fifty-hour weeks, productivity may very well be back down to what would normally be achieved in a standard forty-hour week.

There are at least two reasons for this. One is that people get tired and work output drops. Another is that they sometimes "pace" themselves. As is true in a mara-

Figure 7.4

Bar Chart with Resource Leveling

```
------------------------------ Project description ------------------------------
| Report: Gantt Chart            Date:  1-16-91              Time: 12:09         |
|                                                                                |
| Title: Project Zero            Project ID: SP             Version: 1          |
|                                                                                |
| Manager: Jim Lewis             Project filename: ZERO6    Dept:               |
|                                                                                |
| Project start:  6-17-91        Project end:               Budget:            |
|                                                                                |
| Description:  Small Network to illustrate resource scheduling                 |
|                                                                                |
--------------------------------------------------------------------------------
```

```
------------------------------------ Legend ------------------------------------
| ·····  Activity                    ◆         Milestone                        |
| C····  Activity on critical path   L····     Locked activity                  |
| --···  Partially completed activity  -----   Completed activity               |
| ▲      Original start date          ▼        Original end date                |
| ·····  Discontinuous activity       ·····◆   Baselined milestone              |
--------------------------------------------------------------------------------
```

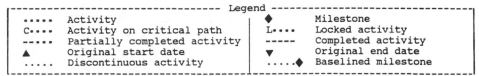

			July 1991						August 1991			
Project Zero	Day	Resrc	17	24	1	8	15	22	29	5	12	19	26

Project Zero	Day	Resrc
Activity A	8	SW
Activity B	18	SW HE
Activity C	3	HE
Activity D	9	SW HE
Activity E	5	SW
Activity F	4	SW HE
Activity G	30	SW HE
Finish	0	X

			July 1991						August 1991			
Project Zero	Day	Resrc	17	24	1	8	15	22	29	5	12	19	26

Resource summary

Utilization

UNASSIGNED		X								
Senior Work	10.0	SW	10.0	10.0	8.0	4.0	10.0	9.0	5.0	2.0
Helper	5.0	HE	1.0	1.6	2.0	4.4	5.0	4.0	0.4	0.6
Total days			11.0	11.6	10.0	8.4	15.0	13.0	5.4	2.6

thon race, if a runner expends too much effort early in the race, he or she may not finish. Workers may also do the same thing, slowing down so they can endure the longer days.

These considerations alone argue against planning projects to be completed using significant levels of overtime to meet required completions. But there is an even more important reason. If overtime is being used just to meet the schedule and problems occur in the project, then there is no room left to compensate. So, as a general rule, overtime should be reserved to deal with unforeseen problems or inaccurate time estimates.

Scheduling With Variable-Duration Activities

As discussed previously, if it is assumed that the duration of work can be shortened by applying more labor, and conversely, then it might be possible to change activity durations and achieve a shorter schedule than is possible when activities are assigned fixed durations. Project Workbench has such a feature.

To illustrate how this works, the activities in the network were changed to variable duration types, but resource availability and resources required for each activity were left unchanged. The new analysis is shown in Figure 7.5.

As the bar chart shows, the schedule is pulled in from an August 7 end date to July 31, an improvement of five days or one working week. This is still not as good as the ideal case, which shows a July 23 end, but it makes more efficient use of resources and time, and would definitely be an improvement.

Note that Activities A, B, D, E, and F have had their durations changed by the computer. Activities A, D, and F are now on the critical path, and Activity D has been split, to allow work to be completed on Activity G (which was originally a critical path activity). The printout shows the new duration for Activity D as seventeen days—meaning from start to finish, rather than working days. The number of working days is only five.

There are some potential problems with this kind of analysis. For one thing, splitting activities almost always causes the total time required to do the work to be

Figure 7.5

Schedule with Variable
Duration Acitvities

```
.------------------------------ Project description -----------------------------.
| Report: Gantt Chart            Date:   1-16-91                  Time: 12:20 |
|                                                                             |
| Title: Project Zero            Project ID: SP                   Version: 1  |
|                                                                             |
| Manager: Jim Lewis             Project filename: ZEROVAR  Dept:             |
|                                                                             |
| Project start:  6-17-91        Project end:               Budget:           |
|                                                                             |
| Description:  Small Network to illustrate resource scheduling               |
|                                                                             |
'-----------------------------------------------------------------------------'
```

```
.------------------------------------ Legend -----------------------------------.
|  .....  Activity                      |  ◆         Milestone                   |
|  C....  Activity on critical path     |  L....     Locked activity             |
|  -....  Partially completed activity  |  -----     Completed activity          |
|  ▲      Original start date           |  ▼         Original end date           |
|  .....  Discontinuous activity        |  .....◆    Baselined milestone         |
'-------------------------------------------------------------------------------'
```

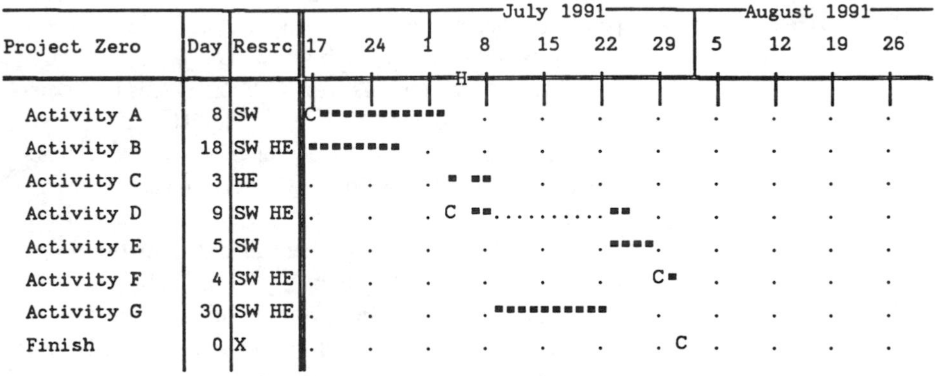

			————July 1991————	————August 1991————
Project Zero	Day	Resrc	17 24 1 8 15 22 29	5 12 19 26
Activity A	8	SW	C■■■■■■■■■■■ . . . .
Activity B	18	SW HE	■■■■■■■■■ . . . .
Activity C	3	HE	. . . ■ ■■ . . . . . .
Activity D	9	SW HE	. . . C ■■..........■■ . . .
Activity E	5	SW	. . . . . .■■■■. . . .
Activity F	4	SW HE	. . . . . . C■ . .
Activity G	30	SW HE	. . . ■■■■■■■■■■ . . . .
Finish	0	X	. . . . . . C . . .

			————July 1991————	————August 1991————
Project Zero	Day	Resrc	17 24 1 8 15 22 29	5 12 19 26

Resource summary

Utilization

UNASSIGNED		X							
Senior Work	10.0	SW	10.0	9.6	6.2	9.4	10.0	9.8	3.0
Helper	5.0	HE	2.0	1.0	2.0	5.0	5.0	3.0	1.0
Total days			12.0	10.6	8.2	14.4	15.0	12.8	4.0

greater than for the unsplit situation. Time is generally lost trying to "get one's bearings," so it is questionable whether this schedule would be feasible.

What is important, however, is that the project manager can conduct these "what-if" analyses in a matter of minutes, rather than discovering after-the-fact that problems exist in the project. Then, using judgment based on experience, the most appropriate solution can be established as the working plan and the project can be run accordingly.

It is important to note that the computer is not *telling* the project manager what to do, but is simply determining solutions based on what data have been presented to it. It is still up to the manager to make a good decision about which solution is best.

Scheduling With Specific Individuals

When resources cannot be considered "generic" or "pooled," the resulting schedule may be different than that obtained when pooled resources are used. Again, using the same network as before, let us assume that two senior-level people are available to work on the project, namely Tom Trump and Sue Simms. In addition, they have a helper named Charlie Clark. They are assigned to work on the project as shown in Figure 7.6.

With these assignments, a standard CPM analysis is conducted. The resource levels under the schedule shown in Figure 7.7 show the loading necessary to complete the project by July 23. Since a level greater than 5.0 represents more than the five working days required in a week, it is easy to see that Sue Simms is overloaded during the week of July 8 and all three are overloaded during the next week.

Next an analysis was conducted using Autoschedule to level resource usage; the result is shown in Figure 7.8. The end date is again August 7, as was determined using pooled resources. The reason for this was simply that the individuals just happen to have been assigned to the project in the same way as was done using pooled people.

If the schedule is studied carefully, it appears that the problem is caused by overloading of Sue Simms.

Figure 7.6

Assignments for Resources

Project description

Report: Activity Detail	Date: 1-07-91	Time: 11:01
Title: Project Zero	Project ID: SP	Version: 1
Manager: Jim Lewis	Project filename: ZERO1	Dept:
Project start: 6-17-91	Project end:	Budget:
Description: Small Network to illustrate resource scheduling		

Original Dates and Usage

Name	Start	End	Duration	Resource assignments	Usage	Cost
			Bus. days	Name		
Activity A	6-17-91	6-26-91	8	Tom Trump	8.0	0
Activity B	6-17-91	7-08-91	15	Sue Simms	15.0	0
				Charlie Clark	3.0	0
Activity C	7-09-91	7-11-91	3	Charlie Clark	3.0	0
Activity D	6-27-91	7-08-91	7	Tom Trump	7.0	0
				Charlie Clark	2.0	0
Activity E	7-26-91	8-01-91	5	Sue Simms	5.0	0
Activity F	8-02-91	8-06-91	3	Tom Trump	3.0	0
				Charlie Clark	1.0	0
Activity G	7-12-91	7-25-91	10	Tom Trump	10.0	0
				Sue Simms	10.0	0
				Charlie Clark	10.0	0
Finish	8-07-91	8-07-91	1	UNASSIGNED		0
Total project	6-17-91	8-07-91	37	Total days	77.0	

Suppose another person were assigned to do Activities E and F, to relieve Sue. Would that solve the problem?

To answer this question, Mary Martin was assigned to the project and allocated only to Activities E and F. When Autoschedule was run using this configuration, only Charlie Clark was overloaded during the week of July 15. If he is removed from Activity F, assuming that Mary Martin can do that task by herself, then an Autoschedule shows that no one would be overloaded, holding the July 23 end date. This analysis is not shown.

However, if Autoschedule is allowed to smooth the use of resources, the program moves the end date out to

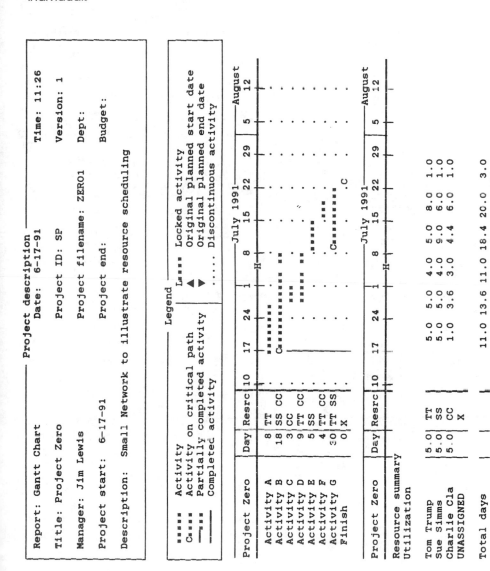

Figure 7.7

Schedule with Specific
Individuals

Figure 7.8

Resources Leveled

```
-------------------------------- Project description -----------------------
| Report: Gantt Chart              Date:  6-17-91              Time: 12:33  |
|                                                                          |
| Title: Project Zero              Project ID: SP              Version: 1   |
|                                                                          |
| Manager: Jim Lewis               Project filename: ZERO1     Dept:       |
|                                                                          |
| Project start:  6-17-91          Project end:               Budget:      |
|                                                                          |
| Description:  Small Network to illustrate resource scheduling            |
|                                                                          |
----------------------------------------------------------------------------
```

```
-------------------------------- Legend ------------------------------------
| ..... Activity                      ♦         Milestone                   |
| C.... Activity on critical path     L....     Locked activity             |
| ----- Partially completed activity  -----     Completed activity          |
| ▲     Original start date           ▼         Original end date           |
| ..... Discontinuous activity        .....♦    Baselined milestone         |
----------------------------------------------------------------------------
```

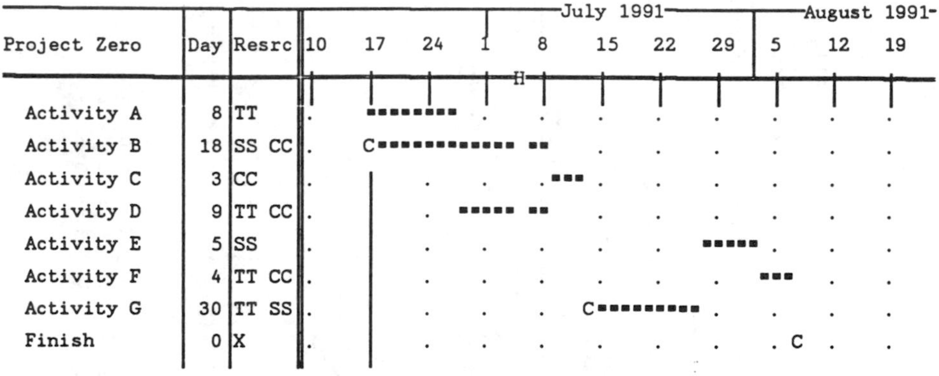

| | | | | | | | July 1991 | | | | August 1991- | |
Project Zero	Day	Resrc	10	17	24	1	8	15	22	29	5	12	19
Activity A	8	TT	.	▪▪▪▪▪▪▪▪	.		.	.	.	.	.	.
Activity B	18	SS CC	.	C▪▪▪▪▪▪▪▪▪▪▪▪ ▪▪	.	.	.	.	.	.
Activity C	3	CC	.	.	.	.▪▪▪	.	.	.	.	.	.
Activity D	9	TT CC	.	.	▪▪▪▪▪ ▪▪	.	.	.	.	.	.
Activity E	5	SS	.	.	.	.	.	▪▪▪▪▪	.	.
Activity F	4	TT CC	.	.	.	.	.	.	▪▪▪	.	.
Activity G	30	TT SS	.	.	.	.	C▪▪▪▪▪▪▪▪▪	.	.	.
Finish	0	X	.	.	.	.	.	.	.	. C	.	.

| | | | | | | | July 1991 | | | | August 1991- | |
| Project Zero | Day | Resrc | 10 | 17 | 24 | 1 | 8 | 15 | 22 | 29 | 5 | 12 | 19 |

Resource summary
Utilization

Tom Trump	5.0	TT		5.0	5.0	4.0	2.0	5.0	4.0	1.0	2.0
Sue Simms	5.0	SS		5.0	5.0	4.0	2.0	5.0	5.0	4.0	
Charlie Cla	5.0	CC		1.0	1.6	2.0	4.4	5.0	4.0	0.4	0.6
UNASSIGNED		X									
Total days				11.0	11.6	10.0	8.4	15.0	13.0	5.4	2.6

July 26. This smooths out everyone's allocation to the project, yielding a level-loaded resource pool, which would no doubt be a bit better for the people actually doing the work. See Figure 7.9.

The project manager would have the option of letting the end date slide about three days or holding it to July 23 and using resources a bit more inefficiently. The important thing is that this solution was arrived at within a few minutes using the computer. Once the various possibilities have been determined, a choice of the most suitable option can be made.

Multiproject Scheduling

The impact of resource constraints illustrated by the single-project example above is magnified in scheduling multiple project - situations where several separate, independent projects are linked together through their dependence upon a pool of common resources.

Project Workbench and other software packages allow the multi-project situation to be analyzed in much the same way as for a single project. Such an analysis is really the only way in which an organization can practically gain control of the multi-project situation when resources are shared among all projects.

A great deal of work is required, but once all of the data has been entered into the computer, project managers have visibility to what is actually possible. They can run projects more efficiently than is possible when resource conflicts are constantly resulting in work being "jerked around," to use the vernacular.

Practical Suggestions for Resource Allocation

In the example analyses presented in this chapter, all workers have been assigned to the project as if they are available to work full time. This is another reason why projects sometimes get into trouble. It is almost never true that a person is available to work on *anything* at a 100 percent rate! There are meetings to attend, non-productive time (such as breaks, goofing off, interruptions, etc.), non-project assignments and a host of other reasons for the loss of availability.

Figure 7.9

Loading with
Mary Martin Added

```
-------------------------- Project description -----------------------
| Report: Gantt Chart           Date:  6-17-91            Time: 12:45 |
|                                                                     |
| Title: Project Zero           Project ID: SP           Version: 1   |
|                                                                     |
| Manager: Jim Lewis            Project filename: ZEROMM  Dept:        |
|                                                                     |
| Project start:  6-17-91       Project end:             Budget:      |
|                                                                     |
| Description:  Small Network to illustrate resource scheduling       |
|                                                                     |
-----------------------------------------------------------------------
```

```
-------------------------------- Legend -------------------------------
| ..... Activity                    |  ◆       Milestone               |
| C.... Activity on critical path   |  L....   Locked activity         |
| ----- Partially completed activity|  -----   Completed activity      |
| ▲     Original start date         |  ▼       Original end date       |
| ..... Discontinuous activity      |  .....◆  Baselined milestone     |
-----------------------------------------------------------------------
```

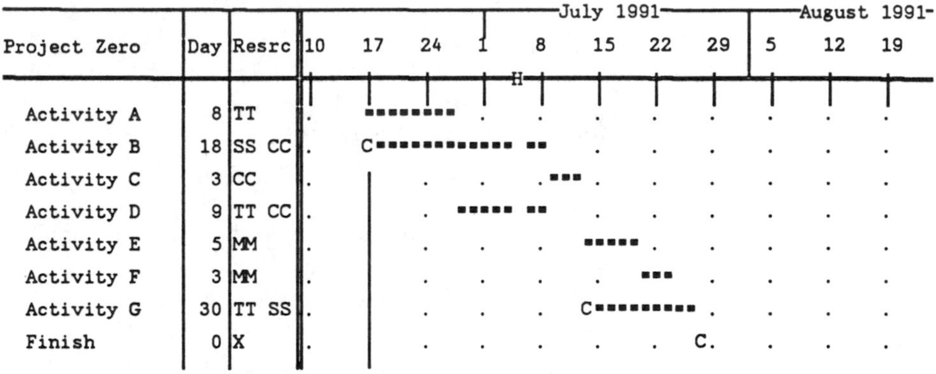

			July 1991 August 1991-
----------------	-----	-------	----10--17--24--1--8--15--22--29--5--12--19--
Project Zero	Day	Resrc	
Activity A	8	TT	■■■■■■■■
Activity B	18	SS CC	C■■■■■■■■■■■■■■ ■■
Activity C	3	CC	■■■
Activity D	9	TT CC	■■■■■ ■■
Activity E	5	MM	■■■■■
Activity F	3	MM	■■■
Activity G	30	TT SS	C■■■■■■■■■■
Finish	0	X	C.

			July 1991 August 1991-
----------------	-----	-------	----10--17--24--1--8--15--22--29--5--12--19--
Project Zero	Day	Resrc	

Resource summary

Utilization

Tom Trump	5.0	TT		5.0	5.0	4.0	2.0	5.0	4.0			
Sue Simms	5.0	SS		5.0	5.0	4.0	2.0	5.0	4.0			
Charlie Cla	5.0	CC		1.0	1.6	2.0	4.4	5.0	4.0			
Mary Martin	5.0	MM					1.0	5.0	2.0			
UNASSIGNED		X										

History can sometimes be used as a guide to determine what percentage of an individual's time can be expected to be available on a project. Activity durations can then be established accordingly. Project Workbench does allow non-project activities to be inserted into a project schedule so that the impact on the project can be assessed. By doing this, a manager can decide if it is best to assign a particular job to a certain individual or whether it would be too great an impact on a project. This permits informed decision-making, rather than having to make decisions based only on "gut reactions."

Resource Allocation Methods

For the reader interested in how computers are programmed to perform resource allocations, a number of references are available. These include Fleming, Bronn, & Humphries; Moder, Phillips, & Davis and specific software manuals, including the one for Project Workbench. See the reading list for titles to the books cited.

Generally speaking, all programs make use of what are called *heuristics,* or "rules-of-thumb," to assign resources. The problem is generally so complex that exact mathematical models are impractical to construct. Moder, et al, present a table of a number of such heuristics. Project Workbench allows the manager to select various allocation rules, which is helpful. While it is outside the scope of this work to describe these in detail, suffice it to say that control of projects can only be achieved if the resource allocation problem is solved, and abundant software exists to help.

Key Points

- When resource limitations are considered, a schedule may not have the float which was determined by standard CPM analysis.

- Resources can be allocated in a "pooled" fashion when they can all do the same work; otherwise, they must be allocated by name.

- The software can show how vacations and holidays will extend working times, so that their impact can be assessed.

- Scheduling can be improved in some cases by allowing activities to be *variable-duration.*

- "What-if" scenarios can be tried quickly with the computer, so that an informed decision can be made about how a project should be scheduled.

- The computer is the only way to gain control of the multi-project resource allocation problem.

The PERT Statistical Approach[1]

Imhotep left the pharaoh's palace and hurried back to his office. He was visibly shaken, walking like a zombie, hardly noticing friends as he passed them on the street. In fact, if he had been capable of hearing, he would have heard several exclaim to their companions, "What's wrong with Imhotep? He looks like he just saw a ghost."

But Imhotep did not hear them. He was so shaken by pharaoh Zoser's new assignment that he was deaf to all outside noises. The thought kept racing through his mind, "Nothing even faintly approaching this monument in size and splendor has ever been created by man."[2]

There had been no preparatory phase, no small pyramids on which to develop experience. In fact, Imhotep thought, only a generation ago Egypt had been a semi-tribal state. Now they were a highly organized society. But this? This was madness. And if he failed... Who knew the bounds of the pharaoh's wrath? And with no experience on which to base his plans, how was he to say with any degree of certainty how long the pyramid would take to construct? He hurried into his office, took out a sheet of papyrus, and began to make sketches. By the gods, he had to do this right!

* * *

Nothing much has changed in the nearly 5000 years since Imhotep faced the biggest challenge of his career. Project managers are still required to plan and estimate jobs for which they have little or no experience to use for comparison. And some of them do encounter the wrath of the "pharaoh" in their own organization if the job is not completed on time and within budget.

We don't know, of course, if Imhotep gave the pharaoh a target completion date (or if one was imposed on him). We do know that the job was of enormous complexity. By the time it was finished, the step pyramid rose to a height of about 60 meters (197 feet) had a base dimensioned 125 by 110 meters (410 by 361 feet) and contained around 850,000 tons of stone. As Men-dels-sohn says:

> [What is] surprising is the realization that the immense technological advance required for pyramid building was not due to a technical revolution. The methods of using stone as a building material and the metal and stone tools employed had been well-known in the Second Dynasty. What was new in Zoser's time was the degree to which all these activities were suddenly escalated. Pyramid-building was a milestone in the history of man because it was his first true application of large-scale technology...The keys to the problem were manpower and *organization.*[3]

When a project consists of activities, most of which are similar to others that have been performed a large number of times, CPM scheduling is generally used.

With CPM, estimates of activity durations are based on historical data, and are assumed to be the mean or average time which the activity has taken in the past.

However, when a project contains a majority of activities for which no experience exists—that is, no historical data is available—then the estimating difficulty becomes significant. Numerous slang terms exist to describe the kind of estimating that is done under this condition, and all of them have to do with the word "guess." When no experience is available to use as a guide, the only thing that can be done is make the best possible guess, based on whatever relevant experience one has.

It seems clear, however, that the more unique an activity is, the less certain the estimate of its duration, and therefore, the *riskier* the project will be in terms of control. And since a lot of projects (such as research and development) fall into this category, the question naturally arises as to whether there might be some method to reduce estimating risk.

In response to this problem PERT was developed around 1958 as a joint effort between the Navy and Booze, Allen, and Hamilton consulting firm and was originally applied to the Polaris submarine project.

While estimates of activity durations for CPM projects are taken as averages based on history, once they are in place, they are often assumed to be more-or-less fixed, or to use the colloquial expression, they are "engraved in granite."

The PERT system, however, is based on the recognition that estimates are uncertain, and therefore it makes sense to talk of *ranges* of durations, and the *probability* that an activity duration will fall into that range, rather than assuming that an activity will be completed in a fixed amount of time.

Empirical Frequency Distributions

To understand the probability and statistics involved in PERT, consider an activity that has been performed in the past many times under essentially the same conditions. For the activity in question, duration times ranged from seven to seventeen days. Now suppose that you count the number of times the activity required seven days to perform, eight days to perform, etc., and you display the resulting information in the form of an empirical frequency distribution or histogram as shown in Figure 8.1.

As we know from statistics, if an infinite number of observations were made, the width of the intervals in this figure approach zero and the distribution would merge into some smooth curve. This type of curve is the theoretical probability density of the random variable. The total area under such a curve is made to be exactly

Figure 8.1

Empirical Frequency Distribution

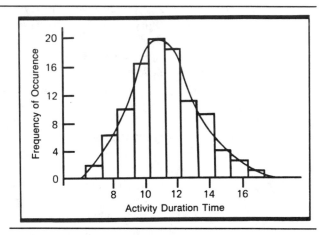

one, so that the area under the curve between any two values of **t** is directly the probability that the random variable **r** will fall in this interval. When this is done, the curve is called a *normal distribution curve*. It is also often called a bell-shaped curve.

Once the normal distribution curve exists for an activity, it is then a simple matter to extract the average-expected-activity duration from the curve and to use that time as the estimate for how long the work will take.

However, under those conditions when no such distribution exists, we could still say that the problem is to arrive at our best approximation of what the average expected duration would be if we *could* perform the work over and over to develop the normal distribution curve. It is the answer to this question which forms the heart of the PERT system.

PERT System of Three Time Estimates

Even though a project may consist of activities for which little or no experience exists, most planners will have some relevant experience, so in most cases it is possible to make an educated "guess" of the most likely time the work will take. In addition, estimates can be made of how long the work would take if things go better than expected and, conversely, if things go worse than expected. These are called the *optimistic* and *pessimistic* conditions, respectively (see Table 8.1).

These three estimates can be thought of as representing aspects of the normal distribution curve that could be developed if the work were performed a sufficient number of times. Another way to think of them is to say they represent information or data about the work in question. Taken together, perhaps a computation of the distribution *mean* can be made.

Table 8.1

Terms Used in PERT Estimating	**Definitions:**
	a = optimistic performance time: the time which would be improved only one time in twenty, if the activity could be completed repeatedly under the same essential conditions.
	m = most likely time: the modal value of the distribution, or value which is most likely to occur more often than any other value.
	b = pessimistic performance time: the time which would be exceeded only one time in twenty if the activity could be performed repeatedly under the same essential conditions.

This is the essence of the PERT system, although what has been presented is an admittedly simplified presentation. The interested reader should consult Moder, Phillips, and Davis (see reading list) for a more thorough treatment of the statistics involved. For our purposes, all that matters is the application of the method.

PERT Computations

In order to combine the three estimates to calculate the expected mean duration for the activity, a formula was derived, based on principles from statistics. The estimate of average expected time to perform an activity is given by the following expression:

$$t_e = \frac{a + 4m + b}{6}$$

where

t_e = expected time
a = optimistic time estimate
m = most likely time
b = pessimistic time

These values of t_e are used as the durations of activities in a PERT network. Given those estimated durations, the network calculations are identical to those for CPM. A forward-pass computation yields earliest times for events and a backward-pass provides latest times.

Estimating Probability of Scheduled Completion

What is gained by PERT, compared to CPM, is the ability to now compute a *confidence interval* for each activity and for the critical path, once it has been located. To do this, the standard deviation of each activity distribution must be known. With PERT software, such a computation would be automatically made by the software. However, if CPM software is used to do scheduling, the calculations can be made externally, perhaps using a spreadsheet (which is very simple to construct, incidentally).

A suitable estimator of activity standard deviation is given by:

$$s = \frac{b - a}{6}$$

where s is the standard deviation of the expected time, t_e.

Once the critical path has been determined for the network, the standard deviation for the total critical path can be calculated by taking the square root of the sum of the variances of the activities on the critical path. Thus, in the case of only three activities on the critical path, the standard deviation would be given by:

$$s_{cp} = \sqrt{s_1^2 + s_2^2 + s_3^2}$$

From statistics, we know that there is a 68 percent probability of completing the project within plus-or-minus one standard deviation of the mean, 95 percent within two standard deviations, and 99.74 percent within three standard deviations. The normal curve is shown in Figure 8.2 for reference.

An Example

To illustrate how PERT works, we will consider a single activity, for which estimates are made by two different planners. The estimates given by each person are shown in Table 8.2, together with the calculated values for t_e and s.

Note that the standard deviation for the estimates made by Person 1 is only 0.5 day, meaning that the spread on the normal distribution curve is quite small. For Person 2, the standard deviation is 1.8 days. For convenience, we will call this 2.0 days even. The normal distribution curve using these two different sets of numbers would look as shown in Figure 8.3.

The impact on the activity estimate is that the *confidence interval* for Person 2 is four times wider than that

Figure 8.2

Normal Distribution

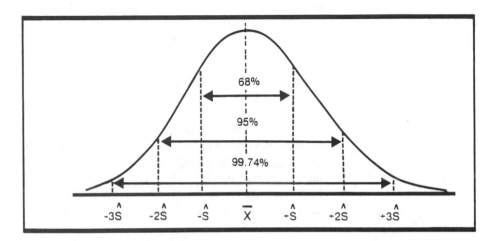

for Person 1 for a given probability of completion of the task.

To illustrate, there is a 68 percent probability that the activity will be completed in the range of 9.7 to 10.7 days if the estimates made by Person 1 were used, whereas the 68 percent confidence interval is 9.5 to 13.5 days if the estimates made by Person 2 were used.

What is meant by these statistics is simply that Person 1 has greater confidence or less uncertainty about his estimates than Person 2. Does that mean he is more correct? No, it is simply a reflection of the different experiences of the two individuals.

Perhaps because Person 2 has had less experience

Table 8.2

Estimates for a Single Activity Made by Two Individuals

Description	Person 1	Person 2
m = most likely	10 days	10 days
a = optimistic	9 days	9 days
b = pessimistic	12 days	20 days
PERT TIME ESTIMATE	10.2 days	11.5 days
Standard Deviation	0.5 days	1.8 days

Figure 8.3

Distribution with Ranges

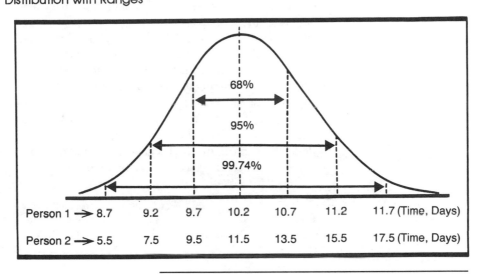

Person 1 ➤ 8.7	9.2	9.7	10.2	10.7	11.2	11.7 (Time, Days)
Person 2 ➤ 5.5	7.5	9.5	11.5	13.5	15.5	17.5 (Time, Days)

with this particular activity than Person 1, he is not sure how long it will take. Therefore, the PERT system would tell him to use an activity duration of 11.5 days as his best estimate of mean duration, whereas Person 1 would only use 10.2 days. This can be thought of as automatically providing some "padding" for the person who has the least confidence in his or her estimates, although I am using the word "pad" here in a different sense than it is normally used.

Using PERT

The fact that PERT requires three-time estimates to be made for each project activity, and that these be plugged into formulas to calculate a time estimate and standard deviation, means additional work compared to CPM. For this reason, many planners consider PERT to be not worth the effort.

In addition, people question the validity of the entire process. They argue that, if all three estimates are guesses, why should the weighted composite of three guesses be any better than just using the most likely estimate in the first place? Indeed, there is merit to this argument. As I see it, one principle advantage of PERT is that it makes everyone realize that durations used to specify the completion of work are not exact, but carry with them *probabilities*.

As was discussed in Chapter Four, it may be better to use DELPHI to arrive at an estimate, or perhaps have several individuals estimate an activity duration independently of each other and simply average them. In any case, the interested reader is referred to the work by Moder, Phillips, and Davis, and to the *Project Management Handbook*, by Cleland and King, for a more in-depth treatment of PERT and probabilistic methods - in project scheduling (see the reading list).

Key Points

- PERT is used when very little experience exists on which to base estimates of activity durations.

- Three estimates must be made for each activity: a most likely, optimistic, and pessimistic estimate.

- These estimates are combined in a formula to yield an estimate of the average expected duration for an activity.

- Standard deviation can then be computed for each activity and a confidence interval can be used to specify the probability that the activity will be completed in a certain range of times.

- A confidence interval can also be specified for the critical path, once it is located in the network.

- A major advantage of PERT may be that it compels everyone to realize that estimates are not exact, but carry probabilities of completion.

Section Four
Project Control

CHAPTER 9 # Project Control and Evaluation

In his book, *The Abilene Paradox*,[1] Jerry Harvey relates
the story of Captain Kohei Asoh, a Japan airlines pilot,
who, on November 22, 1968, landed his DC-8 jet, with
96 passengers and 11 crew members on board, two-and-
one-half miles out in the San Francisco Bay, but in
nearly perfect alignment with the runway on which he
was supposed to land. According to Harvey, Captain
Asoh landed the jet so smoothly that many of the passengers were unaware that they were in the water until
someone pointed out a sailboat floating nearby. No one
was injured, not even bruised, and they were all extri-
cated from the plane and ferried safely to land in
inflatable life rafts.

The inevitable hearing was convened by the National Transportation Safety Board (NTSB) shortly

afterward, and everyone expected Captain Asoh to be hung up by his toes in downtown San Francisco, totally disgraced.

Captain Asoh was the first witness called to testify, and as he took the stand, all eyes and ears were attuned to the battering he was certain to endure. The investigator opened the hearing with the obvious question, "Captain Asoh, in your own words, can you tell us how you managed to land that DC-8 Stretch Jet two-and-a-half miles out in San Francisco Bay in perfect compass line with the runway?"

Captain Asoh never hesitated. His reply was straightforward and honest. "As you Americans say, Asoh f..k up!"

With that, the inquiry was essentially over. All that remained was to tidy up details. What more is there to do when the accused admits his guilt?

Harvey calls this the "Asoh defense," and suggests that it should be invoked more often. Certainly, when things go out of control, when Murphy's Law works its wrath on managers, the Asoh defense may make more sense than trying to cover one's behind.

It certainly worked for me. At one point in my career, when I was a young, inexperienced project manager, I sent a set of drawings to our machine shop to have some prototype parts made. The machinist screwed them up, and they wouldn't work. When I asked him why he had botched a relatively simple machining job, his reply was essentially the Asoh defense.

"Because I'm a dumb ass," he said.

With that, there was nothing more to be said, except, "Well, do them over and make them right this time."

Concept of Control

One of the primary responsibilities of a project manager is to ensure that things are done as they are supposed to be done—in other words, that control of a project is maintained. As was true for Captain Asoh, landing the plane in San Francisco Bay is unacceptable, and bringing a project in late and over budget is similarly taboo.

In short, a project manager is expected to meet the *good, fast, cheap* objectives discussed in Chapter One. If this is to happen, proper project control is necessary. Therefore, the design of a project control system is very important. However, before the system can be designed, it is essential to understand the basic concepts of control by answering the questions in Figure 9.1.

To repeat the definition offered in Chapter One:

> Control is achieved by comparing where one is with where one is supposed to be, then taking corrective action to resolve any discrepancies which exist.

Although the word *control* often refers to power, authority, command, or domination, the definition offered above is more like what is involved in aircraft or marine navigation. The pilot is guiding a vessel by comparing his or her course to the planned route in order to arrive at a predefined destination.

The central idea in this meaning of control is that *information* is used to maintain satisfactory progress toward a desired goal. This definition invokes the model for a basic *feedback system* and is the model that should be applied to project control systems. A simple feedback system is shown in Figure 9.2.

This way of looking at control in terms of information processes, rather than in energy terms, is helpful because it leads to insight into how a manager must deal with people. When control is thought of in terms of energy or power, it inevitably leads to authoritarian management, in which the manager tries to achieve control by closely monitoring workers and giving orders for them to follow. Such a control method is ineffective for at least two reasons.

For one thing, the manager is burdened with having to closely monitor workers, which does not give him much time to do anything else. Thus, planning and other management activities tend to suffer. Further, such a method of control is not very effective if a number of

Figure 9.1

Concept of Control

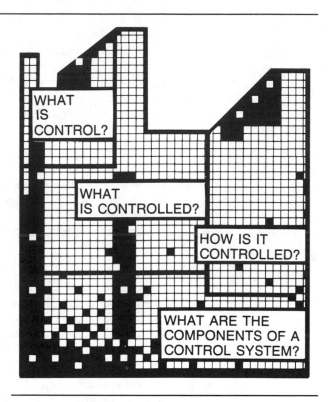

Figure 9.2

First-Order Feedback
System

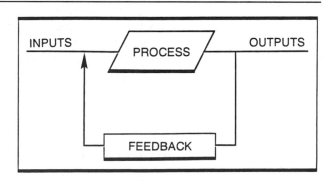

workers must be monitored, since the manager cannot easily practice surveillance on all of them at once.

The second reason why authoritarian management does not work well is simply that today's worker does not readily accept it. People today expect more autonomy, and do not willingly let managers treat them like pawns. However, when they do accept authoritarian management, they absolve themselves of responsibility for the outcome of their efforts. As long as they do what they have been told to do, if the outcome is unacceptable, they can respond to the manager with, "Well, I did what you told me and it didn't work. What do you want me to do now?"

For these reasons, a manager must ultimately establish a situation in which workers achieve self-control, so that work is controlled—not workers. The objective must be to get the work done, not make workers perform in lock-step fashion. Attempts to constrain and regiment workers generally lead to resentment and an atmosphere that stifles creativity, which is just the opposite of what is needed. Control should be viewed as a tool that the worker can use to work more effectively and efficiently.

Consider for a moment the word *organization*. It has the same root as the word *organism*. The human body is an example of a complex organism. If any organ of the body does not function correctly, the entire organism suffers. In the same way, if any member of a project team does not function correctly, it will have an adverse effect on the entire project. Therefore, we can say that:

> A manager is only in control if every member of her team is in control of his or her own work.

The best way to see this is to consider the words *macro* and *micro* control. The project manager is interested in achieving macro control of the project. That is, at the top level of the Work Breakdown Structure, the project is supposed to be in control. Following the WBS model, we can think of the Work Package or Level-of-Effort as points where micro control is exercised. Clearly, if micro control is not achieved, no macro control will exist, since top level control depends on what is happening at the lowest levels of the project. The individual must be in control of his or her own work so that micro control will exist.

The term most often used to designate what the manager must achieve is *empowerment*. Employees must be empowered to do their jobs with the minimum supervision that is consistent with the individual's capability. Enabling individual members of a project team to achieve self-control is absolutely essential if real project control is to be accomplished.

In order to show how this can be achieved, a Standard Operating Procedure (S.O.P.) for empowering people is presented in Table 9.1. Each point is explained below.

1. The first step is to be sure that each team member is clear on what his or her objective is. As pointed out in Chapter Three, a statement of objective must be understandable. Ideally, the team member involved would participate in the development of those objectives, so that clarity is automatically achieved.
2. Each team member must also have a personal plan that will determine how his or her objective is going to be achieved. Again, it is most helpful when each member has participated in planning the project at his or her level of involvement.
3. The project manager must be sure team members have all the resources needed to do the job. These include tools, equipment, and supplies or material. In addition, the individual must have the necessary skills to do the job or must be given training. It may be necessary to include in the project budget the expense of providing team members training in specialized areas for which no training budget is normally provided by the overall organization.
4. Feedback must go directly to the person doing the job *from the work itself*—not back through some circuitous route, such as the Management Information

Table 9.1

How to Empower
People

S.O.P. for Empowering People

The employee needs:
1. A clear definition of what he or she is supposed to be doing.
2. A personal plan on how to do the required work.
3. Skills and resources which are adequate.
4. Feedback on progress which goes directly to the person from the work itself.
5. A clear definition of his or her authority to take corrective action when there is a deviation from plan. And it cannot be zero!

System (MIS). If you have ever had the experience of driving while someone navigated for you, and about three seconds after you passed a turn they told you about it, you know how frustrating such an experience is. It all boils down to not being in control! You didn't have the map, and the road signs meant nothing to you, so you couldn't exercise control.

In an analogous way, one of the major problems with MIS is that by the time information flows through the system to tell about a deviation from plan, it is too late to make a smooth correction. You have already "missed the turn," and must now backtrack. This is not to say that MIS is not useful. It is useful for overall checks-and-balances, but not for micro-level control.

5. Finally, the individual must have a clear definition of his or her authority to take actions to correct for deviations from plan, and that authority must exist! If the individual has no control, the manager does.

Naturally, there will be limits. The normal method is to say that so long as the person is within a certain percent tolerance around the target (such as plus-or-minus ten percent) she is to correct for those small deviations herself. On the other hand, if she finds the deviation exceeds the ten-percent limit, she must consult with her manager and they will jointly decide what to do about the problem.

Why Control Systems Sometimes Fail

While the procedure presented above is sound, it will not function in a climate of fear, distrust, or antagonism. When people know that they will be punished for making mistakes, they will first play it safe. They are unlikely to invoke the Asoh defense.

This ultimately means that they won't do much of anything innovative, because that increases risk. Further, if they play it safe and still have problems, they will then try to hide them until the problems become too big to hide.

Much has been written on the need to establish an organizational climate that fosters openness, honesty and innovation, and it is outside the scope of this book to fully address the subject. Tom Peters has a great deal to say in his book, *Thriving On Chaos*, about how to promote good working relationships, and his points are relevant to project teams as well. It must be remembered that project management is not just a set of tools, it is a discipline, and the "bottom line" is that success is only possible if people are managed properly.

Components of a Project Control System

The feedback system shown previously is a very simple one, which systems people call a *first order* system. It is not very elegant, and has some serious limitations as a model on how to achieve control in project management.

For those readers unfamiliar with feedback systems, a good analogy for the first-order system is the thermostat in one's home. In the winter, the system provides heat and the desired room temperature is preset by adjusting the thermostat to the proper level.

It should be clear that every system is designed to work properly only under certain conditions. For example, the home heating system might be designed to maintain the room at seventy degrees Fahrenheit so long as the outside temperature does not go below minus thirty degrees. When the outside temperature drops below that level, the heater will run continuously, but the room temperature will begin to drop below the pre-set level of seventy degrees.

To maintain the desired room temperature, the system would have to increase its heating capacity, but it cannot do this. Thus, it keeps running without being able to adequately heat the house.

In a similar manner, a project may run into unexpected obstacles that fall outside the boundaries for which the project control system was designed. For example, everyone is following the plan to the letter, but they are not getting the desired result. What is needed is to change the approach. However, a first-order control system does not have that capability. Something more flexible is needed. The third-order system shown in Figure 9.3 is the answer.

The system in Figure 9.3 has the same basic elements as the first-order system of Figure 9.2. There are inputs, processes, outputs, and feedback. However, the third-order system feeds information about the system outputs to a *comparator*, which weighs them against the original plan. If there is a discrepancy, that information is passed to an *adjust* element, which must decide if the discrepancy is caused by something being wrong with the process, the inputs or the plan itself.

Once that determination is made, the adjust element calls for a change in the plan, inputs or the process. Note also that the adjust element has an arrow going back to the monitor. If a deviation is detected, the monitoring rate is increased until the deviation is corrected, then monitoring is decreased to its original level.

The real-world analogy is that if you were monitoring progress on a project weekly and a problem occurred, you might begin to monitor daily. If the problem becomes serious enough, your monitoring rate might increase to several times each day. Once the problem has been solved, you would revert to your weekly monitoring.

Comparing performance against plan can be difficult when the work cannot be quantified. How do you know what percentage of a design is complete, for example? Or if you are doing a mechanical drawing of a part,

Figure 9.3

Third-Order Feedback
System

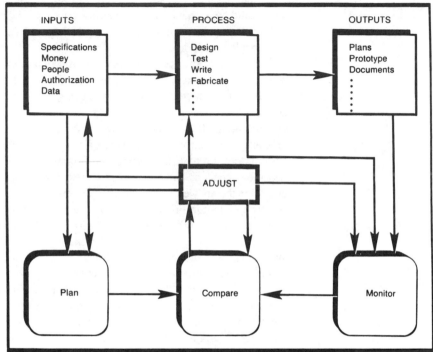

Source: Adapted from Claude Burrill and Leon W. Ellsworth,
Modern Project Management (Tenafly, NJ: Burrill-Ellsworth
Associates, 1980).

is the drawing 75-percent complete when 75-percent of
the area of the paper is covered? Probably not. Measuring progress in *knowledge work*, to use Peter Drucker's
term, is very difficult.

This often leads to strange results. Suppose a member of the project team has agreed to design a new golf
club, and has promised to finish it in ten weeks. At the
end of week one, she reports that the design work is 10-
percent complete. At the end of week two, the work is
20-percent complete. In week three she hits a small snag
and gets a little behind, but by week four she has caught
up again. Figure 9.4 shows a plot of her progress.

Everything goes pretty well until week eight when she hits another snag. At the end of that week, she has made no progress at all. The same is true the following week, and the following and the following...

What happened? For one thing, the 80/20 rule got her. In the case of knowledge work, it says that 80 percent of the work will be consumed by 20 percent of the problems encountered, and they will always happen near the end of the job.

> I still have checks—I must have money in the bank!
>
> —Cathy

The real issue, though, is how she measured progress in the first place. Chances are, at the end of the first week, she reasoned somewhat like *Cathy* in the comics and said to herself, "I'm at the end of the first week on a ten-week job. I must be 10-percent complete." And she would be in good company, because that is exactly what a lot of people do when *estimating* progress on knowledge work.

Note the word *estimate!* Assessing progress when work is not easily quantifiable is estimating and is an subject to all the difficulties discussed in Chapter Four. This shows the limits of our ability to achieve control in management.

It is for this reason that two practices are advisable. First, work should be broken into small "chunks" that permit progress to be monitored fairly frequently, perhaps in intervals no greater than two weeks. Second, tangible deliverables should be used as signposts to show progress. In design, a drawing is tangible evidence of progress. The same is true with software development. Printed code or written functional specs are evidence that work is complete. Having it "in one's head" is impossible to verify.

Figure 9.4

Percent Complete
Report

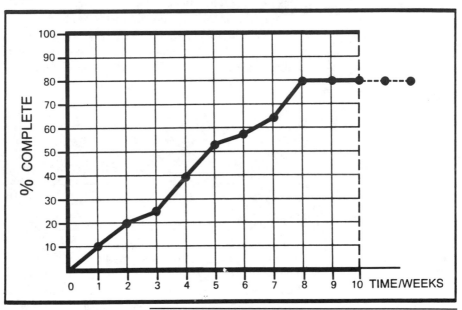

Using Variance or Earned Value Analysis in Project Control

Even though there are limits in assessing exactly how much work has been done on a project, there can be no control unless some assessment is done. The most widely used method of measuring project progress is through *variance* or *earned value* analysis.

First, we define variance as follows:

Variance: any deviation from a plan

Variance analysis allows the project manager to determine "trouble spots" in the project and to take corrective action. As was mentioned previously, there are three areas of the project which the project manager is expected to control. These are the *good, fast, cheap* objectives. Because of the difficulty of quantifying the performance objective (good), variance analysis is usually not applied, but only to the cost and schedule targets. In that case, the project manager will have to monitor the quality targets, using whatever standards can be developed, and take necessary steps to ensure that they are met.

As for the schedule and cost objectives, the following terms define what is to be monitored:

- **Cost Variance:** Compares deviations only from budget and provides no comparisons of work scheduled and work accomplished.
- **Schedule Variance:** Compares planned versus actual work completed. This variance can be translated into the dollar value of the work, so that all variances can be specified in monetary terms.[2]

In order to make cost and schedule variance measurements, three variables are used. They are defined in the following paragraphs, together with examples of how they are calculated.

- **Budgeted Cost of Work Scheduled (BCWS):** The budgeted cost of work scheduled to be done in a given time period, or the level of effort budgeted to be performed in that period. This is the *target* toward which the project is headed. Another way to say it is that BCWS represents the *plan* which one is supposed to follow. It is basically the product of man-hours and the dollar labor rate that is paid during a given period of time, usually a day or week at a time.

  As an example, suppose that a project is to employ two people working on the project for one week (forty hours) at the labor rate of thirty dollars per hour each (loaded labor—with overhead included). In addition, a third person will work on the project for thirty hours during the same week, but at a loaded labor rate of fifty dollars per hour. The budgeted-cost-of-work-scheduled for the week, then, is the sum of two products:

40 hours x 30 $/hour x 2 = 2,400 dollars
30 hours x 50 $/hour x 1 = 1,500 dollars
BCWP Total: 2,400 + 1,500 = 3,900 dollars

- **Budgeted Cost of Work Performed (BCWP):** The budgeted cost of work actually performed in a given period. BCWP is also called *earned value.* It is a measure of how much work has been accomplished.

    The BCWP figure is calculated as follows. For the example above, assume that the two employees who are assigned to work for a full forty hours each actually put in that amount of effort. One worker actually gets her work complete, while the other does not. He only completes about 80 percent of the work supposed to be done. The worker assigned to put in only thirty hours also completes his work as planned. We say that the *earned value* of the work completed, then, is as follows:

    40 hours x 30 $/hour = 1,200 dollars
    0.8 x 40 hours x 30 $/hour = 960 dollars
    30 hours x 50 $/hour = 1,500 dollars
    BCWP Total: = 3,660 dollars

- **Actual Cost of Work Performed (ACWP):** The amount of money actually spent in completing work in a given period. This is the amount of money paid to workers (wages only—no material costs are included in any of these figures) to do the work that was completed during the time period in question.

    To continue with the above example, assume that the work completed has actually cost the organization $3,900. If this figure were compared with BCWS, we might think the project is in good shape. The scheduled work was supposed to cost $3,900, and that is what has been paid in labor. However, we also know that one person did not get through with the work he was supposed to do. The value of his accomplishment is only $960, but was supposed to be $1,200. In order to see what this means for the project, the following formulas are employed:

    Cost Variance = BCWP - ACWP

Schedule Variance = BCWP - BCWS
(Dollar value)

Plugging numbers into these formulas, we have the following results:

Cost Variance = $3,660 - $3,900 = -$240

A negative cost variance means that the project is spending more than it should—thus, a negative variance is *unfavorable*.

Schedule Variance = $3,660 - $3,900 = -$240

Again, a negative schedule variance means that the project is behind schedule, and so is also *unfavorable*.

Looking at these two figures together tells us that the project has gotten behind schedule in the amount of $240 worth of work, and since the cost variance is identical to the schedule variance, we know that the cost variance is due only to the schedule variance. That is, the work being done is costing what it was estimated to cost. If labor rates had escalated, then the cost variance would be greater than the schedule variance.

Variances are often plotted using spending curves. Figure 9.5 is a BCWS curve for a project. It shows the *cumulative spending* planned for a project and is sometimes called a *baseline plan*. Such curves can often be plotted automatically by transferring spending data from a scheduling program (which calculates labor expenses on a daily or weekly basis by multiplying labor rates times manpower expended) to a graphics program using a DIF file or some other file-transfer format.

Consider the curves in Figure 9.6. On a given date, the project is supposed to have involved $50,000 dollars (50K) in labor (BCWS). The actual cost of the work performed (ACWP) is 60K. This figure is usually obtained from the accounting department and is derived from all of the time cards which have reported labor applied to the project. Finally, the budgeted cost of work performed (BCWP) is 40K. Under these conditions, the project would be behind schedule and overspent.

Figure 9.5

BCWS Curve

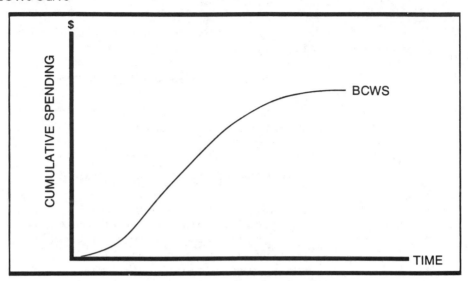

Figure 9.6

All Three Curves

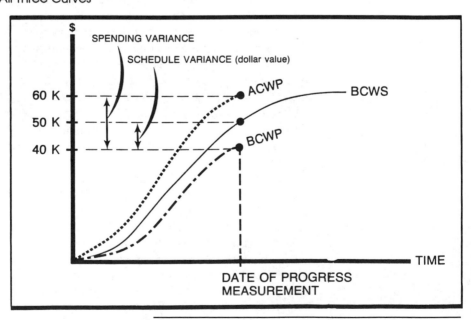

To understand this, the project has spent 60K to accomplish only 40K worth of work. That means an overspend of $20,000. The plan called for 50K worth of work to be done, but they have only completed 40K worth, so they are behind schedule as well.

Figure 9.7 illustrates another scenario. The BCWP and ACWP curves both fall at the same point, 60K. This means that the project is ahead of schedule, but spending correctly for the amount of work done. To see this, the project has spent 60K and has accomplished 60K worth of work. However, the plan called for 50K worth of work, so the status is ahead of schedule.

Is there any potential problem with being in this position? At first glance, no. However, if you consider how a project can be in this position, you find that more resources must have been applied than were planned, but at the planned labor rate (since there is no spending variance). Where did the project manager get the extra people? In most environments, resources are shared, so

Figure 9.7

BCWP and ACWP at
Same Point

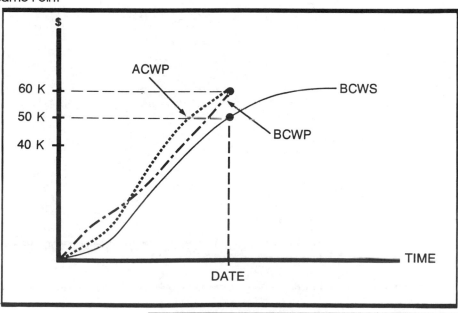

it may be that this project is ahead of schedule at someone else's expense.

Another consideration is cash flow. While the project is ahead of schedule, can it be funded at the rate being spent? If not, then the work would have to be decelerated.

The next set of curves illustrates another status. In Figure 9.8 the BCWP and ACWP curves are both at 40K. This means the project is behind schedule and underspent. This project is probably starved for resources (the victim of another project manager being ahead). Labor is costing what it is supposed to cost, but not enough work is being done to stay on schedule. The problem for this project manager is that she will probably go over budget in trying to catch up, since premium labor will most likely be required.

Finally, Figure 9.9 looks like Figure 9.6, except the ACWP and BCWP curves have been reversed. Now the

Figure 9.8

BCWP and ACWP
Below Plan

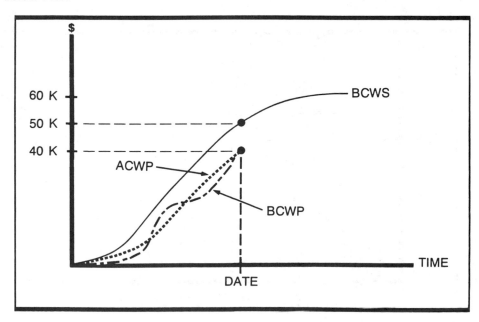

project is ahead of schedule and underspent. The accomplished work has an earned value of 60K, but the actual cost of that labor has been only 40K. There are three possibilities that could explain how this project manager achieved the result shown.

1. Actual labor rates were considerably lower than expected, and the people were more efficient than anticipated.
2. The project team had a "lucky break." They had expected to have to work really hard to solve a problem, but it turned out to be very easy.
3. The project manager "sand-bagged" his estimates. He padded everything, playing it safe.

If you believe the first situation, you will believe anything. It is very unlikely that both variances would happen at the same time. The second situation happens

Figure 9.9

Ahead of Schedule,
Below Budget

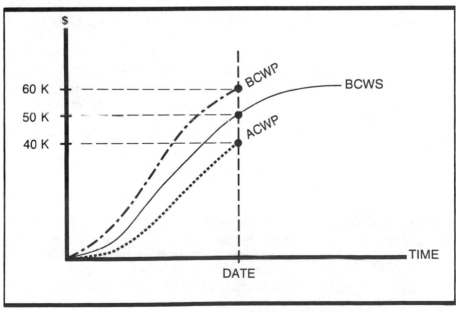

occasionally. When all the planets are aligned—about once in a zillion years—you say, you bet!

The third situation is the most likely explanation. The project manager was playing it safe. And he would tell you that there is no problem. After all, the project will come in slightly ahead-of-schedule and underspent, which means he will give money back to the company. No problem. The controller no doubt has the budgeted funds in an interest-bearing account, so the company is earning interest on the money.

Right. But banks are not known for being overly generous with interest, and there is a rule that says that if you can't make a greater return on an investment than the interest a bank will pay, you should go out of business and just put your money in the bank. You don't need the aggravation of being in business, and you aren't very good at it anyway.

As a matter of fact, the economists would say that there is a real *opportunity cost* involved in this project. The company has lost an opportunity to get a good return on its investment because the money was budgeted for this project, and therefore could not be used anywhere else. This is another problem with padding.

The question is, naturally, what is reasonable? We certainly cannot expect to have zero variances in a project.

However, there is no easy answer to the question. As was mentioned in Chapter Four, well-defined construction projects can be held to very small tolerances—as small as plus-or-minus three percent. Research and development projects are likely to run higher tolerances, perhaps in the range of 15 to 25 percent. Each organization has to develop acceptable tolerances based on experience.

Refining the Analysis

The only problem with the analysis presented here is that it is an *aggregate* figure, and does not specify the area in which a problem exists; it may even hide a problem completely. For that reason, the variance analysis needs to be conducted on a task-by-task basis.

This is usually done at the Work Package level, but it can be at any level of the WBS at which one wishes to track project progress. By summing the individual Work Package figures, the aggregate figure can be used to gauge the overall "health" of the project, while a line-by-line accounting can be used to spot specific problem areas.

The importance of this was brought home to me by a client who reported that they had been using aggregate analysis to gauge project status for some time, and they discovered that a $100,000 overspend in one area of a project was being counter-balanced by a $100,000 underspend in another area. It looked like the project was in good shape, but such huge variances indicate a lack-of-control that should be addressed. By using a form such as the one in Figure 9.10, such problems can be avoided.

Variance thresholds can be established that define the level at which reports must be sent to various levels of management within an organization.

By combining cost and schedule variances, an integrated cost/schedule reporting system can be developed.

The Need for all Three Measures

Occasionally project managers fall into the trap of trying to track their projects using only BCWS and ACWP. As long as they see no difference between what they had planned to spend and what has actually been spent, they think the project is running smoothly. However, we saw from the previous examples that this may not be true, and the manager would not spot a problem until it had perhaps gotten serious.

In fact, a controller from one organization told me that he constantly sees this happen in his company. For a long time the project goes along being underspent or right on target. Then the project manager realizes that the work is not getting done as required, and a big effort is applied to catch up. The usual result is that spending overshoots the planned target. This is illustrated by the curves in Figure 9.11.

Figure 9.10

Tracking Form

PROJECT STATUS REPORT

Project #	Description		Date
			Page _____ of _____
Prepared by:		Signed	

WBS #	Cumulative To-Date					At Completion		
	Budgeted Sched.	Cost Work Performed	Actual Cost	Variance Sched.	Variance Cost	Budgeted	Latest Est.	Variance
TOTALS								

Figure 9.11

Overshoot Curve

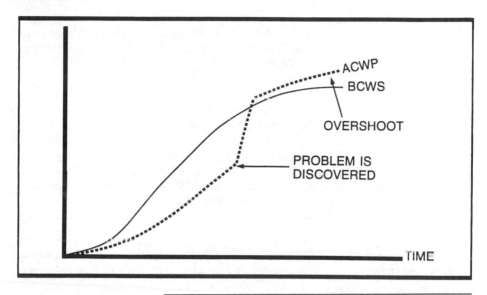

Variance Analysis Using Hours Only

In some organizations, project managers are not held accountable for costs, but only for the hours actually worked on the project and for the work actually accomplished. The argument used to justify this way of working is that project managers usually have no control over labor rates. This is because an individual may be assigned to the project by his or her functional manager simply because he or she was the only person available who could do the job, but his or her rate is 25 percent higher than what the project manager expected to pay when original estimating was done.

The other cause of problems is that the accounting department may change burden allocation rates (for valid reasons), which causes total labor costs to go above original estimates. This naturally creates a cost variance in the project, but one over which the project manager has no control, and so the argument is that he or she should not be held accountable.

In this case, the same analysis can be conducted by stripping the dollars off the figures. This results in the following:

BCWS becomes Total Planned (or Scheduled) Hours
BCWP becomes Earned Hours (Scheduled Hours x Percent Work Accomplished)
ACWP becomes Actual Hours Worked

Using the new numbers, it is possible to compute the following variances:

Schedule Variance = BCWP - BCWS = Earned Hours - Planned Hours
Labor Variance = BCWP - ACWP = Earned Hours - Actual Hours Worked

True Project Cost Versus Apparent Cost

The shape of a cumulative spending curve for a project is a function of how labor is applied. The typical curve has a soft *S-curvature*, which occurs because the initial phase of work is preparatory in nature and only a few people can get started at once. Then the work accelerates and finally tapers off near the end of the project as "loose ends" are wrapped up. However, other shapes are possible. Figure 9.12 shows three possibilities.

Curve A is the typical curve. Curve B is obtained when resources are allocated linearly to the project—that is, resources are level-loaded. Curve C shows what happens when the project is back-end loaded. There is a long period in which the work progresses slowly, then accelerates. Note that all three curves result in the exact same total project cost at the end.

However, they all have advantages and disadvantages. Curve A would be useful when the organization gets progress payments for work completed. Curve B would be an advantage when cash flow is a problem.

Curve C would be helpful if some preliminary work must be done to decide whether to scrub the project or continue. Assuming that the decision could be made in all three scenarios, if the project were cancelled, the differences between points where the curves intersect a vertical line would represent the different losses that

Figure 9.12

Three Possible Spending
Curves

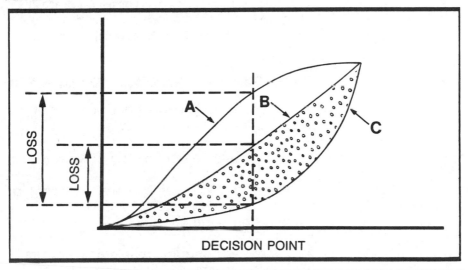

would occur. Naturally, the losses would be smallest
with Curve C.

The next point that is important is to consider the
area between any two curves. For example, the area between Curves B and C has been shaded. The units on
that area are dollars multiplied by time, or the *time-
value-of-money*. We have a special name for that
product. It is called *interest!* Therefore, the area between any two curves represents the difference in the
cost of capital for each project.

In the case where progress payments are being re-
ceived, that interest advantage would be obtained with
Curve A. The money comes in fast and the company
can invest it.

When money is being borrowed, however, the interest advantage would be obtained with Curve C. The
money is held as long as possible, then spent rapidly.

The problem with Curve C, however, is that back-
end-loading a project increases risk of being late.
Chances are always good that problems will occur near
the end of a project, and if it is already loaded heavily to

meet a deadline, there may be no chance of adding resources to deal with last-minute problems.

The point of all this is that by allocating resources to a project correctly, the project manager can actually affect the *true cost* of the work, even though the *apparent cost* would be the same for several different plans.

Key Points

- Control should be thought of in terms of *information*, rather than power.

- Work should be controlled, not workers.

- People should be empowered by applying the standard operating procedure provided in the chapter.

- People will not admit problems if they are punished for having them; therefore, innovation will be sacrificed.

- A third-order feedback system is the best model for use in project control.

- Variance or earned-value analysis permits the manager to assess project status, but it must be done at the work-package level in order not to hide problems.

- Variances can be in terms of dollars or hours.

- By allocating resources correctly, a project manager can affect the true cost of work.

Section Five

Project Organization

CHAPTER 10 Developing the Project Organization

An organization is a group of people who must coordinate their activities in order to meet their objectives. (Note the similarity to the definition for a team.) Coordination requires good communication and a clear understanding of the relationships and interdependences among people. There is no *single best* organization structure; rather, the form used must be one that optimizes performance by balancing human (or social), reward, and technical requirements (see Figure 10.1.)

Every organization consists of three central components, as shown in Figure 10.1. These components are related to each other in such a way that if one changes, it affects the other two.

A good example of this was the introduction of personal computers into organizations in the early 1980s.

Figure 10.1

Components of an
Organization System

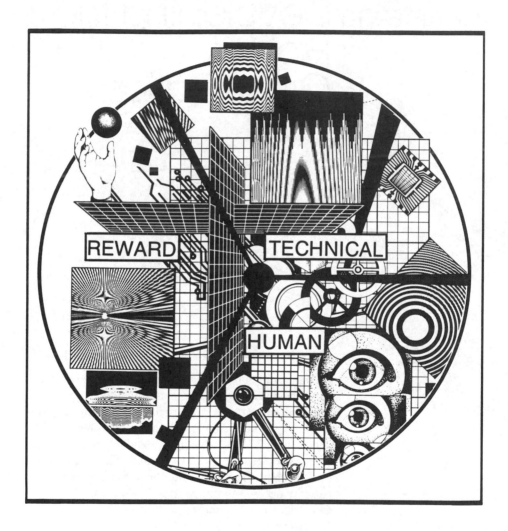

The impact has been enormous. Not only have people changed the way in which they interact, but the reward system in many organizations has changed as well. People who would not or could not become computer literate have, in some cases, found themselves "stuck" in dead-end jobs. They cannot advance or get pay raises as high as their peers who have gained computer skills.

The personal computer has also made it possible for people to do work at home, which formerly would have required them to be at the office to do. They can even work while in hotels and planes, making their productivity even greater than before.

But there are negatives as well. The computer has changed our concept of time. When I first started teaching seminars on how to use personal computers in project management, we were using the original Visi-Calc™ spreadsheet, mostly on Apple II computers. Initially, people voiced a lot of "Wow!" and "Look at that!" comments as they watched the speed with which the computer could recalculate the row and column totals in a spreadsheet. Within three years, they were saying, "Darn, this thing is really slow!"

Jeremy Rifkin discusses this in more detail in his book, *Time Wars*.[1] Because of this change in our concept of time, we tend to want everything yesterday, and this is certainly pertinent to our concept of how long it should take to complete various activities in a project.

The point of this discussion is that the three components of an organization must be managed as well as the project itself. And since these three components will be affected by the form of organization chosen, then making the best choice is important.

Organization structure is dictated by communication needs together with such factors as technology and its rate-of-change, task complexity, resource availability, the nature of products and services being provided, competition and decision-making requirements.

The *formal* organization is the one defined by the organization chart, which is established and sanctioned by company management. The *informal* organization, however, consists of the everyday relationships and communication patterns that exist among people, which may differ considerably from the formal structure. It may, in fact, be more important in determining where the company goes than the actual formal structure. The project organization is the one shown by a Linear Responsibility Chart.

The formal structure must provide each individual with a clear understanding of the authority, responsibility and accountability given so that his or her work can be accomplished. (See Figure 10.2.)

- **Authority** is the power granted to individuals so that they can make decisions that others are expected to follow. Authority is usually conferred by one's position.
- **Responsibility** is the obligation for which individuals have to perform their assignments effectively.
- **Accountability** is the responsibility an individual assumes for the satisfactory completion of a specific assignment.

In Chapter Nine, a standard operating procedure was presented for empowering people, and it was pointed out that no person can exercise control unless he or she has some authority to take corrective action when there is a deviation from a predetermined target. In addition, this section pointed out that people do not accept responsibility for the result of their actions if they are managed in an authoritarian way. As long as they do what they are told, they are not responsible, if the outcome is not the one desired. Rather, they feel that the person whose orders they were following is responsible.[2]

A consequence or corollary of this is that those people will also not take any initiative. They finish one thing and wait to be told what to do next.

The lesson to be learned from all this is that we cannot delegate responsibility without also delegating authority commensurate with it, but organizations try to do so all the time.

Traditional Organization

The traditional organization structure is a hierarchical form with a single manager at the top, to whom middle

Figure 10.2

Authority, Responsibility,
and Accountability

managers report. This line of reporting relationships continues downward to the lowest level of the organization.
This form continues to be the predominant structure
used in most organizations. Figure 10.3 illustrates an example of the traditional form applied to a project.

There are some definite advantages to organizing a
project in hierarchical form. Because the members of
the group report to the project leader or one of his or her
staff, loyalty is to the project, rather than to some other
part of the company. Communication channels are well
defined, and there is good control over personnel, since
each employee has a single boss. This means that a manager has flexible use of personnel.

On the other hand, if the project group is fairly
small, and there are several disciplines involved, problems are created by the hierarchical structure. For
example, I am an electrical engineer. If I were to set up
a project in hierarchical form, and if there were one programmer in the group, I would have a problem, since
my knowledge of programming is very limited.

I would be unable to evaluate the quality of the programmer's work, and I would have no idea if his

Figure 10.3

Hierarchical Organization

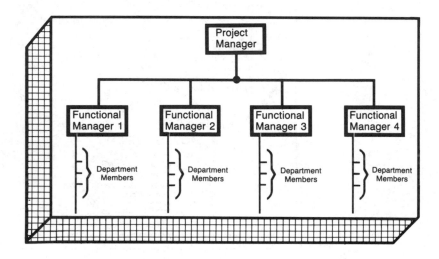

estimates of activity durations were reasonable or not. In addition, if I only had about enough work to keep the person busy for 85 percent of the time, I would have to pay his full-time salary but only get an 85-percent return on my investment.

In addition, consider what happens when the programmer has difficulty with a technical problem. There may be no one else in the group to help him. If he were located in a group of programmers, he would be able to call on them to help.

It was for these and other reasons that other forms of project organization were tried in the 1950s and 1960s, culminating in a form that has become almost synonymous with project management. This is the *matrix* form, shown in Figure 10.4.

Figure 10.4

Matrix Organization

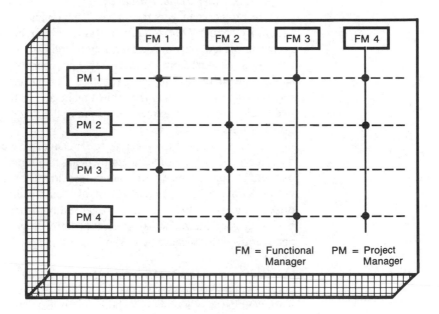

FM = Functional Manager   PM = Project Manager

Matrix Organization

The matrix form is intended to take advantage of pure functional structure in achieving the needs of a multi-disciplinary project. It is ideally suited for companies, such as construction, that are "project-driven."

A primary reason for using the matrix form is given by the answer to several questions. "Why should it be necessary to physically remove a technical person from her functional group? Why not leave her in her group and let her supervisor, who is herself a technical specialist in that discipline, worry about the quality of this person's work, her day-to-day work assignments, and so on." Indeed. Why not?

The matrix form leaves a company organized along functional lines (programmers, chemists, electrical en-gineers, carpenters, plumbers, accountants, and so on in their own functional departments). As projects are set up, people are drawn from those departments on an as-needed basis. The functional departments are shown in Figure 10.4 as having solid lines running vertically, a simplified illustration of the *vertical lines of authority that exist in a hierarchical structure.*

The project managers then have dashed lines of "authority" running horizontally across the hierarchical organization, and the dots at intersections indicate that a person (or persons) from the department above is assigned to work on the project as required. The dashed line is used to indicate that the project manager has limited (really no) authority over the person in the functional group.

This means that the project manager cannot give orders to people and "enforce" them by using his authority over the person, because he has none. Instead, he must get work done using *influence.* A rule-of-thumb is that a project manager who has a matrix organization better have very good interpersonal skills, together with good negotiating skills because he or she is going to need them!

In the end analysis, of course, we have already pointed out that authoritarian management does not work well in today's society, so both the project manager and the functional manager need good interpersonal skills.

Making Matrix Work

It is generally agreed that matrix organization is the only way to "fly" in managing projects, but such a form is extremely difficult to manage. Because people from each functional department are shared among a number of projects, there are always conflicts in which the same individual is needed on two or more projects at once. There are conflicts caused by disagreements about how work should be done. And there are problems caused by the fact that individuals assigned to a project really have their primary loyalty to their functional department, and not to the project.

In my experience, several important issues must be attended to if a project manager is going to be successful in a matrix organization. First, the relationship between the project manager and functional managers is absolutely vital to cultivate. I don't mean that a project manager must go out and drink beer with a functional manager every afternoon, or even socialize with him or her at all, for that matter.

What I mean is that a project manager must be on good terms with functional managers, should understand what makes them "tick," should understand their values and their ways of thinking, and should work to establish a relationship of respect with them.

To put it bluntly, if a functional manager "hates your guts," and you need that manager to go a little beyond the "call of duty" for you, then you are in trouble.

Second, since resources are shared across all of the projects in an organization, if a project manager sees that her work is going to slip, which means that people from a functional department won't be needed when originally planned, then she should advise the functional manager immediately! It is a difficult-enough job to juggle resources across a number of projects without being caught unaware on Monday morning by a project manager who announces that she doesn't have any work for those people as she had planned.

Third, project managers should have input to the performance appraisals which are written by functional managers on their people. This is one way to gain some commitment and loyalty to the project on the part of functional department members.

Finally, a project manager must be able to remove any person from her project who can not or will not perform satisfactorily. Since they were hired by functional managers, a project manager cannot fire people from the organization, but she must be able to "fire" them from the project. Otherwise, how can she be held accountable for the overall project work?

I know that this is idealistic in some respects. I have lived with it first-hand. When a functional manager is told that a person is not performing and that you want someone else, he may say, "He's all I have to give you. Take him or leave him."

When that happens, the only recourse is to make the best of it or appeal to a higher authority in the organization and let them intervene. In any event, dealing with a problem employee in a matrix organization is a real problem and one for which there are no easy solutions.

Key Points

- An organization is established to coordinate the work of a number of people.

- The organization consists of human, technical and reward systems. A change to one of these will affect the other two.

- Hierarchical structure has serious disadvantages for running multi-disciplinary projects.

- Matrix is almost synonymous with project management because of its advantage in dealing with many disciplines.

- Success in matrix requires very good interpersonal skills on the part of all managers.

CHAPTER 11 Staffing a Project

The way in which a project is staffed depends upon the type of organization structure being used. In a hierarchical project organization, team members may be hired into the company for specific assignment to the project itself. They may also be recruited from functional groups already existing in the company. Either way, they are "hired" to work only on a single project. In the matrix organization, the functional manager usually determines which specific personnel will be assigned to a project on a strictly as-needed basis. Those individuals still "belong" to their functional manager, not to the project manager.

In the hierarchical-project setup, also called "pure-project" form, determination of how many people in each skill category are required for a project may be

solely the project manager's job, while it would be nego-
tiated in the matrix.

The Staffing Process

Naturally, the first step is to determine what must be
done. The WBS is the tool used to show exactly what
tasks will be involved in the project. Once it has been
developed, it is possible to decide what kind and how
many people from each skill category must be used on
each task.

In some organizations, project managers might be
able to decide what organizational form will be used,
whether matrix or hierarchical. Usually, however, that
decision has been made by top management and is established as a standard. If a choice can be made, it should
be done at this point.

If matrix is used, functional managers will assign individuals to the project. Often project managers have
preferences for certain individuals, either because they
are known to do good work or the project manager has
worked with a person before and likes working with
him. It may be possible to request that person and get
him, but in a shared-resource environment, that may
only be possible in the event that the person is the *only*
one who can perform a certain task. Otherwise, functional managers generally are pretty free to assign
personnel on an availability basis.

If the project manager has any say about who is assigned to the project, he may need to interview and
select people. If so, there are some guidelines for conducting interviews following this section of the chapter.

If possible, when matrix is the organization form,
have people assigned to the project before final planning
is complete, so that they can participate in preparing
those plans. In this way, they will feel greater commitment to the plan than if it is just handed to them as a *fait
accompli.*

In any event, work hard to get the person selected
started off on the right foot. If the person is very inexperienced, they will need a lot of "hand-holding" at first.
Regardless of experience level, all members of the team
need to have very clear understanding of the project ob-

jectives and the approach being taken to get there. The success or failure of a project may well depend on how the project is "kicked off."

Selection Interviewing Guidelines

Too many managers do all of the talking during a selection interview. You can't learn anything about the other person if you're talking. Ask open-ended questions as much as possible—those which require that the person elaborate, rather than just giving you "yes-no" answers. Following are some examples of what you might ask:

- What are the greatest strengths you think you would bring to this job?
- What accomplishments during your career do you feel best about (work or non-work)?
- What new skills have you developed recently?
- What did you do to increase your responsibilities or improve your job in your last position?
- What level of supervision makes you most comfortable?
- Will you be able to meet the particular requirements of this position (e.g., travel, overtime, weekend work, heavy deadline pressure, etc.)?
- Besides economic rewards, what do you look for in your work life?
- What could I tell you about this position or the organization to help you determine if this is the right job for you?

You can also ask how the prospective employee would handle various situations. For example, "If the general manager came directly to you and gave you a work assignment, how would you handle the situation?"

Tell potential hires both the good and bad (or negative) aspects of the job. Studies have shown that when employees are told only good things about a job, they feel surprised and perhaps a bit cheated when they begin to discover the negatives. The ultimate result is depressed motivation, and in many cases, turnover. If you oversell the position, chances are you can't deliver and the new employee will feel cheated.

Don't use esoteric interviewing methods unless you have been thoroughly trained in them.

Key Points

- The starting point for staffing a project is the WBS.

- Once tasks have been identified, decide what skill-level person will be required.

- Ask open-ended questions in an interview, so that the applicant does most of the talking.

- Don't use esoteric interviewing techniques unless you have been thoroughly trained in them.

Section Six

Managing People, Politics, and Relationships as a Project Manager

The Role of the Project Manager

The previous chapters of this book have presented the tools of project management. These tools are necessary, but not sufficient condition for success as a project manager. Skills in dealing with people must be added. After all, except for very small, one-person projects, the job of the project manager is to get work done by other people.

During the week prior to revising this chapter, I taught a three-day class in project management for a group of twenty-four engineers. These young men all graduated from engineering schools within the past two years and joined my client company. They are finishing a year-long training program, of which the project management class is just one part.

To use an understatement, the discussion about the project manager's role became very animated at times.

Most of my classes on project management are attended by more experienced people. This class, however, made me realize just how difficult the project manager's role is for a new manager, and showed me how inexperienced individuals view that role initially. I decided to use that class as the basis for this chapter, and I am indebted to my participants for their questions, challenges and understandable skepticism, all of which forced me to think through the issues in detail.

In discussing the control of projects, I presented the standard definition of control which has been given in this book: Control is comparison of where you are to where you are supposed to be, then taking action to correct for any deviation.

"We can't take corrective action," they told me. "We don't have any authority over the people who work on our projects."

Of course, this is why I have written in Chapter Nine that a manager only has control if his or her people are in control of themselves, and that those people must be empowered using my Standard Operating Procedure, so that they are able to exercise self-control.

"The people can't even do that," they argued. "If they need to buy something or work overtime, our policies and procedures require that such actions be approved by someone else, so they can't act unilaterally."

What they said is true. However, it misses an important point. Just because an action must be approved by someone else does not mean that it cannot be taken. Nor does it absolve the individual of the responsibility for getting that approval.

What impressed me about this expression on their part is that they, like so many individuals in organizations, feel *powerless* to act at all. There is a certain paralysis that sets in when a problem exists. It can be explained in part by the widespread use of authoritarian management for so many years, in addition to authoritarian parenting and teaching.

People have been told what to do by their parents, teachers and supervisors for so long that they have come to view the world as a place in which they have no power to affect their own lives. Thus, instead of being proactive, they become reactive, and view the organization (and world) as tying their hands so that they cannot exercise control, even when they are managers.

Now that the problem has been recognized, enlightened managers are trying to correct it. We are trying to adopt more participative styles, and we are trying to empower people. Self-managed work teams represent one such attempt to give the worker more control over his or her work and eliminate authoritarian practices.

Unfortunately, the initial reaction to such a move is distrust. "They're up to something," the worker says. "They're just trying to get more work out of us without paying us any more."

There is also confusion. In one organization, a man told me, "I've been working here twenty years. During that time, when I came to work, they wanted me to hang my brain on the front gate. Now they want me to carry the whole load."

That sums it up as poignantly as any expression I have heard. Hang your brain on the gate. We don't want you to think. Just do what you're told.

Now they suddenly want him to think, but his brain is still hanging out on the front gate.

The same message is often given to new managers, like the young men in my class. "We want you to manage this project," they are told. "It's your baby, and you are responsible for seeing that it comes in on time and on budget." Then they are told, "But don't do anything drastic without checking with me first, and if you want to buy something, we have to get my signature, my boss's signature, the plant manager's signature...and if it's for more than 5000 dollars, it will have to be signed by the president."

By such practices, new managers are given double messages. "You are in control," says one message. "But don't do anything without checking first," says the other. This contradictory communication results in the feeling of powerlessness for those new managers. So it is no wonder that the fellows in my class were a bit confused.

However, my response was this: While it is true that you do not have direct authority to control many aspects of your project work, you must take steps to break roadblocks by appealing to those individuals who do have the authority to act.

Furthermore, it seems to demonstrate that the "power" of authority is misunderstood. People think that if they only had authority, they could move mountains. They argue that the organization will not give them any authority, and therefore, they cannot move even a tiny ant hill.

What they don't realize is that, even if they had authority, it would not guarantee that people would automatically do what must be done. As I have already said, authoritarian management leads to difficulty. So even if they had authority over people, it would not guarantee compliance, nor would it be the best way to work. What must be used is interpersonal skills to get things done. That means *influence*.

In support of this, one of the participants told me that he works hard at building relationships with people in the plant. He gets to know them. He finds out how they think, what they like to do in their free time, and so on. Then when he needs to get something done, he requests it as one friend to another, and he usually gets cooperation.

Yet his boss views his small talk with those people as a waste of time, which is true of a lot of managers. "We're here to work," they say, "not to socialize." Still, this young man is able to get things done that his boss cannot accomplish.

As for the matter of the organization not giving a manager any authority, I learned early in my career that you have as much authority and responsibility as you are willing to take. The manager who *exercises* authority—that is, makes decisions, behaves proactively and who takes responsibility for his or her actions, is the one who eventually rises to the higher levels of the organization. The manager who "cries in his beer" that he can't get anything done stays where he is.

There is a saying which conveys this idea nicely. "It is always easier to ask forgiveness than to get permission." That is the essence of the proactive manager's attitude.

Some simple examples will illustrate the point. In most organizations, requisitions for purchased parts, equipment and tools must be signed by an approving individual. I asked them if those individuals ever "sit on" their requisitions.

"It happens all the time," they all chimed in.

"What do you do about it?" I asked.

"Just wait until they sign it," several of them said.

"Then you aren't managing the project," I told them. "You're just being reactive. You have to let that person know that the requisition must be signed by a certain date, or the following consequences will result: The project will be late; it will cost the company so many dollars; the customer will cancel the order; there is a penalty clause in the contract; or whatever the result will be."

"You have to keep pestering him until that requisition is signed or he throws you out of his office and tells you not to bother him any more. Then, if he does that, you revise your schedule to show the impact of the delayed items, and publish it. That is your responsibility."

"And polish up your resume," someone chirped.

We all had a good laugh. Then we admitted that there are definitely some risks. Nothing comes without a cost—or at least a potential cost.

Another issue that was discussed is the difficulty of managing a project when someone in another department does not act as required by the project plan. The project manager has no authority to tell that person what to do. However, if the success of the project depends on that person's performance, and the manager is unable to influence that person to get moving, then the only recourse is to enlist the help of someone in the organization who can gain that individual's compliance, even if it is through the use of authority. To simply sit around and say, "My project was late because they didn't do their work as planned," is an unacceptable response if the project manager took no action to deal with the problem.

Then someone in the session asked, "What am I supposed to do when someone does not do their part on time?"

"In the first place," I told them, "if someone is supposed to deliver something to you by a certain time, it is your responsibility to be checking with them ahead-of-time to see how they are doing. There should be no last-minute surprises. You should know in advance that they are going to be late, and should be taking steps to prevent such schedule slips by working with those people to do whatever is necessary. If they need more help, you have to 'lobby' with other managers to get that help. If it is a technical problem, you may have to pitch in and help them solve it. Again, at the expense of sounding like a stuck record, it is the proactive approach that is necessary."

Dealing With Resistance

One of the more common complaints from managers is that other departments are sometimes difficult to deal with. They won't cooperate. They build boundaries around themselves and refuse to cross them.

Invariably, when I ask the person who complains about resistant people, "What's in it for them to do what you want done?" they have no answer. They have usually not taken the time to find out what is important to the other person, and all they care about is getting their job done.

The macho manager would say, of course, "What's in it for them is keeping their jobs. That's why they should cooperate." That response, however, is based on contempt for people at the worst, or a failure to understand basic psychology at the least. People do what they do because they get something out of it. So to fail to help others get what they need in the process of doing what you need done is to be very unrealistic in your expectations. The savvy manager knows this and tries to be sure the person will get a fair exchange in the interaction.

Sometimes the refusal to cooperate is caused by the people in the department feeling threatened. To illustrate, one project manager told me that his company had a problem with high scrap rates, which were costing the company several-hundred-thousand dollars a year. He was given the assignment to determine the primary cause of the high scrap.

He designed an experiment in which half of the raw material was held aside and the other half was run through process one, which was very carefully controlled. Then the material was sent through the subsequent processes and the scrap level was measured.

A few weeks later, the remaining material from that lot was run through process one, which was again carefully controlled, then it was put through the remaining steps. The scrap rate was considerably higher than before. This proved that the material was not the cause of the problem, nor was process one. The cause was in the subsequent steps.

When he pointed this out, he got a very defensive response. Naturally, the people who performed those steps were being told that they were doing something to cause high scrap rates, and they did not want to admit it, because people do not like to be "blamed" for errors.

Here again, this is an outcome of our traditional way of dealing with people. Instead of blaming and punishing people for problems, which does not solve the problem, we must enlist their support in solving those problems. Otherwise, people hide problems or resist changing their ways, since to do so would be to admit that what they were doing was wrong.

What I suggested to this manager was to adopt a new approach the next time. "People don't argue with their own data," I told him. "If you can run the same experiment next time, with them totally involved in the design, implementation and *interpretation of the data,* and then ask them how to solve the problem, you won't be as likely to get much resistance." It will be their data and their interpretation. People don't argue with their own data.

The Need for Flexibility

All of the foregoing should reinforce the need for a project manager to have good people skills, and because she must deal with so many different people, all of whom have different personalities and dispositions, she must have a great deal of flexibility in her approach. The same is true when solving non-people problems. A person must be flexible in his or her methods.

Most managers think they are fairly flexible. They believe they are able to change their approach to solving a problem if the first method fails to work. On the contrary, I have seen a number of managers get trapped into simply using "more-of-the-same" in dealing with a problem which does not yield to the first "attack." The problem with this is explained by the Law of Requisite Variety.

Law of Requisite Variety

> In any system of men or machines, the element in the system with the greatest flexibility in its behavior will control the system.
> —Ross Ashby

Consider the system diagram in Figure 12.1. The system involves a process that converts inputs into outputs and uses feedback to keep the process functioning as required. This system model can be applied at the interpersonal level, in which the process involves the interaction of the project manager (element A) with the rest of the project system (element B). Of course, the manager wants to ensure that the element represented by B does what is required. That is, he or she wants to be in control of the outputs from the system.

The law of requisite variety says that the element inside the system (A or B) that has the greatest flexibility (variety) will control the behavior of the system. So if the manager is to control, he or she must have greater flexibility than the remainder of the elements that make up the project system.

A corollary of the law can be stated as follows:

> If you always do what you've always done, you'll always get what you've always gotten.

Figure 12.1

Feedback System

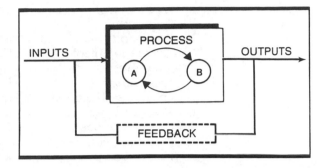

This is almost the opposite of the old adage "If at first you don't succeed, try, try again." We might say instead:

> "If you try repeatedly and don't succeed—try something different!"

Developing flexibility is a life-long task. Only when we have a big "bag of tools" at our disposal can we hope to be able to deal with all of the situations we are sure to encounter.

Unfortunately, rather than develop flexibility in themselves, too many managers attempt to reduce the variability in the system. They do this by imposing rules on the people in the organization. These are usually called *policies* and *procedures*.

In order to maintain control, they try to limit the behavior of the people who report to them. The net result is the one which we have discussed. People begin to feel powerless (which is exactly the intent of the policy, when you get right down to it). For this reason, Tom Peters[1] has argued forcefully for the need to get rid of the myriad of policies that serve only to strangle the organi-

Table 12.1

Attributes of Project
Managers

	Good listener	Visible leadership
	Supportive	Technical knowledge
	Organized	Fair
	Clears road blocks	Flexible
	Mutual respect	Open-minded
	Team builder	Delegates
	Knows own limitations	Honest/trustworthy
	Sense of humor	Understanding
	Gives feedback	Challenges team to do
	Good decision-maker	well
	Follows up	Knows strengths/ weak-
	Shares experience	nesses of team mem-
	Mutual ownership	bers
	Buffer to rest of organiza-	
	tion	

zation, and instead to give employees more autonomy. I agree with him wholeheartedly.

Attributes Required of Project Managers

As a summary of what is required of a project manager, I have asked people in my classes to list what they think it takes to make a good manager. In Table 12.1 is a list which contains some of the more significant characteristics listed by those participants.

Key Points

- A project manager must be proactive.

- You have as much authority and responsibility as you take.

- Authoritarian management causes people to feel powerless.

- People don't argue with their own data.

- A project manager must have flexibility.

CHAPTER 13 Leadership in Project Management

In Chapter Twelve it was pointed out that authoritarian practices are ineffective in managing projects. On top of that, the project manager seldom has authority over many of the people assigned to the project anyway, so he cannot practice authoritarian management. If he tries under those conditions, he is likely to incite a rebellion. If he is to succeed, he must have the ability to deal effectively with people. This certainly involves leadership, in addition to other interpersonal skills.

What Is Leadership?

The term "leader" is used very loosely in organizations. Dozens of books have been written on how to practice leadership. The topic has been widely researched and numerous definitions exist, many of them not very satisfactory. It seems obvious (though it is often over-looked) that no one is a leader unless he or she has fol-lowers.

In addition, not all managers are leaders, even though they are supposed to be exercising leadership as a normal part of their jobs. Perhaps it is this fact that causes some observers to say that we have a crisis in leadership in our country today.

To *manage* means to handle. To *lead*, by contrast, means to take someone to a destination. We manage things, but we lead people. In my opinion, Vance Packard summed up what we mean by leadership with the following definition.

Definition

> Leadership appears to be the art of getting others to want to do something that you are convinced should be done.
> Vance Packard, *The Pyramid Climbers*

How you get people to *want* to do something consti-tutes the practice of leadership, and is the focus of this chapter.

To determine how leaders influence their followers, Kouzes and Posner conducted an extensive study of leaders and documented their findings in a book entitled *The Leadership Challenge*.[1] They write that leaders ap-pear to adopt a three-phase strategy in getting people to follow them, which they call VIP—vision-involvement-persistence. Leaders have dreams or *visions* of what could be. They also recognize that they can not get there alone, so they work to create *involvement* of others. Fi-nally, they are *persistent* in working toward their goal. (See Figure 13.1.)

The Practice of Leadership

Kouzes and Posner say that vision, involvement, and persistence are expressed through five fundamental prac-tices that enabled the leaders they studied to get extraor-dinary things done. When they were at their personal

Figure 13.1

The Practice of
Leadership

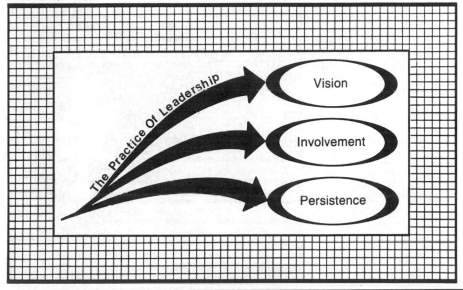

best, those leaders practiced the steps shown in Figure
13.2.[2]

Challenging the Process

Kouzes and Posner[3] say that every case they studied in
which a person performed at their personal best involved some kind of challenge. It might have been a
business turnaround, some innovative new product, or
whatever, but there was always a change in the status
quo. Rather than be satisfied to let things continue the
way they had always been done, these leaders pushed
for a new way.

Inspiring a Shared Vision

James McGregor Burns, in his study of political leaders,[4] pointed out that people only follow someone who
they believe can take them to a destination that they
want to reach. Another way of saying this is that they
must see something of value in following the other person—they must have some of their needs met.

A sense of purpose, mission, or vision creates a
great motivation in people, and leaders are able to create

Figure 13.2

Kouzes' and Posner's
Steps

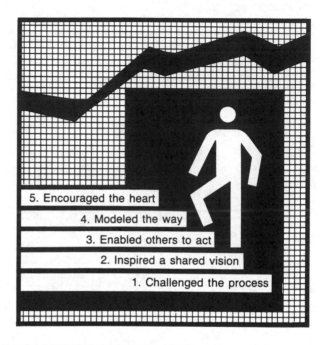

5. Encouraged the heart
4. Modeled the way
3. Enabled others to act
2. Inspired a shared vision
1. Challenged the process

such a shared vision. As Kouzes and Posner say, "A person with no followers is no leader, and people will not become followers until they accept a vision as their own. You cannot command commitment, you can only inspire it."[5]

Gail Sheehy supports the importance of a sense of purpose. In her book *Passages*, she reports that she surveyed some 60,000 Americans and found that those who were most happy, contented and productive had some over-riding sense of *purpose* in their lives—something bigger than themselves—that drove them. Leaders are able to bring such a sense of purpose alive for their followers.

Enabling Others to Act

A number of years ago David McClelland studied the motivations of corporate executives and found that the need for power is a dominant driving force among those individuals.[6] However, McClelland found that the power motive can be expressed in two ways—the *personal power* motive and the *social power* motive.

He argues that the most effective leaders are those who appeal to what he called the social power motive, which is expressed as the drive to do things together. In today's vernacular, we would say that such leaders *empower* their followers. Rather than tie their hands through domination and restriction, effective leaders make people feel stronger.

Reinforcing McClelland's position, Kouzes and Posner say that there is a one-word test to determine whether someone is on the way to success as a leader. That word is *we*. Leaders can't do it alone.

Some leaders try, however. McClelland found that ineffective leaders are inclined to use the personal power motive, which is characterized by the word "I." These leaders tend to be authoritarian, self-centered, and insensitive to the wants and needs of their followers.

By listening to leaders talk, McClelland found that you can tell which power motive they generally adopt. You hear the word "we" with those leaders who have social power as a driving force, whereas the word "I" predominates for the others.

The Chinese sage Lao Tse knew about this aspect of leadership and described it several thousand years ago, as quoted below.

The Way of Subtle Influence

Superior leaders are those whose existence
        is merely known;
The next best are loved and honored;
The next are respected;
And the next are ridiculed.

Those who lack belief
Will not in turn be believed.
But when the command comes from afar
And the work is done, the goal achieved,
The people say, "We did it naturally."[7]

Modeling the Way

Effective leaders lead by example. They are role models for their followers. They practice what they preach, and they also live their values. Employees are very quick to point out the discrepancies between a manager's stated values and his or her behavior. When a manager's behavior is not consistent with his or her stated beliefs, people ultimately will lose respect for the manager.

Encouraging the Heart

Difficult objectives can cause people to become frustrated, exhausted, and disenchanted. Leaders must encourage them in order to keep them from giving up. The leader has to show them that they can win. In addition, leaders must give themselves encouragement.

The Self-Fulfilling Prophecy

The self-fulfilling prophecy is one of the most important principles from psychology, at least for leaders. The principle is that you tend to get what you expect from others. Thus, if you expect poor performance from a person, you will tend to get it, and conversely.

Support for the Self-Fulfilling Prophecy

A well-known account of the experiments that indicated that the self-fulfilling prophecy might be valid was published by Rosenthal and Jacobson.[8] Children were given aptitude tests, and were then paired up according to test scores, race, and sex. Thus, two black boys having equal scores would be paired, and so on. Their teacher was not told the actual test scores. Instead, for each pair of children, the teacher was told that one child was average, while the other was a "late bloomer." The average child would do all right in school, but the late bloomer could be expected to do really well that year. So the teacher was told.

Later that school year, academic performance of the children was checked, and the late bloomers were found to be doing better, on the average, than their counterparts. The only logical explanation for this is that the teacher somehow brought about the expected performance based on the bias presented by the experimenter. But how was this done?

Subsequent studies showed that teachers were more supportive of the late bloomer, more helpful, offered more encouragement, and were more patient when the late bloomer was having difficulty. Thus, the child per-formed better because the teacher expected it. The average child was not so strongly encouraged, and so did not work as hard as the late bloomer. Thus, the self-fulfilling prophecy comes true.[9]

It Works in Management, Too!

Based on this principle, McGregor developed a manage-ment model which suggested that the views which man-agers have of employees might bring about such a self-fulfilling prophecy. He believed that the supervisor's view of employees can be called a "working theory" about employees, and that such views can be placed on a continuum, on one end of which is the Theory-X posi-tion, with Theory-Y on the other.

The Theory-X manager thinks employees are poorly motivated, lazy, interested only in pay, and so on. The Theory-Y manager sees employees as moti-vated, interested in their jobs, etc. This is shown in Figure 13.3. In other words, it is the opposite of the The-ory-X view. According to McGregor, the manager who holds a Theory-X view of employees will tend to get poor performance from them and vice versa.

While this theory is generally correct, I feel that it needs clarification. It is tempting to view the leader as having unidirectional influence in the interaction with followers, whereas the influence is really *bidirectional*. That is, the follower influences the leader and is also in-fluenced by the leader. This is shown in Figure 13.4.

No doubt the reason that the self-fulfilling prophecy works in the classroom is that the strength of the teacher's influence is greater than that of the student. In the workplace, however, the supervisor does not always have greater influence on employees than they have on him. For that reason, the supervisor's expectations do not always bring about the predicted result.

In my experience as a manager, I found the X-influ-ence seemed to be a bit stronger than the Y-influence, so that the X-employee eventually causes the supervisor to lose his normal Y-outlook. However, it is a matter of degree. If the supervisor can maintain a Y-outlook in the face of an employee's X-behavior, then he or she may "turn around" that employee. Certainly, one is generally likely to get better results with the Y-outlook than its opposite.

Actions Speak Louder Than Words

As was previously mentioned, a leader who espouses one thing and then behaves inconsistently with the stated position will not be believed or trusted. For that reason, you cannot *fake* a Theory-Y outlook. You can't tell your followers that you trust and have confidence in them when you don't, because your behavior will contradict your words. For example, if you really don't trust someone, you will let them know it by looking over his or her shoulder fairly often, asking questions that convey your distrust, and in many other ways.

Organizations tend to convey a Theory-X or Y outlook in the policies and procedures that they establish. To illustrate, consider that most adults can make major purchases on their own volition (perhaps in consultation with their spouse, of course). They do not have to obtain permission from their parents to buy a new car or house, which might amount to many thousands of dollars.

That same individual, however, finds that she cannot spend fifteen dollars of the organization's money without permission from the "powers-that-be." (These are our organizational parents!) Heaven forbid! She might spend that fifteen dollars unwisely, and after all, you can't expect management to meet profit objectives if every person in the company can just spend money willy-nilly.

Interestingly, managers will tell employees that they must have approval to spend fifteen dollars, and in the very next breath tell them that they must all behave *responsibly!* Isn't that incredible? If you treat people as though they are irresponsible, how can you expect them to behave responsibly?

It seems to me that the way to deal with this problem would be to give every employee who might have the discretion to spend money her own individual budget. After all, the organization essentially has to create such a budget anyway. Each employee costs the company so much to support, so why not let the person have her own budget and hold her responsible for it! So

Figure 13.3

Theory X, Theory Y

Figure 13.4

Bidirectional Influence

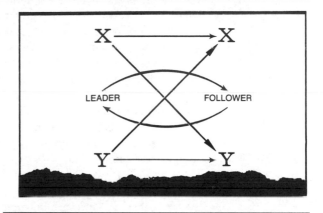

long as she spends the money wisely, she can spend it any way she chooses, in support of her job. If she proves herself untrustworthy, then her manager should deal with her individually, rather than making a policy to tie the hands of everyone.

In Chapter Fourteen, when motivation is discussed, it will be clear why I am advocating this. For now, suffice it to say that the best way to get people to behave responsibly is to treat them as if they are. The self-fulfilling prophecy works in all arenas of life.

223

Choosing a Leadership Style

Of course there must be controls. There must be accountability. Certainly a manager cannot just turn everything over to the follower. The question is, how is a manager to know just how to supervise an employee? Should the person be supervised closely? Would a participative style be best? Or could delegation be employed?

I think the answer is provided by a model of leadership developed originally by Hersey and Blanchard,[10] which I have modified using my own terms. Their model was based on the fact that there are two primary components in the *behavior* of leaders toward their followers.[11] One is the emphasis which leaders place on getting the *task* done. The other is how they deal with their followers in terms of interpersonal or *relationship* dimensions. These are defined as follows:

Task behavior is communication on the part of a manager aimed at the task itself. When task behavior is high, the supervisor defines the follower's role, tells the person what, when, how and where to do the job, and then closely supervises performance.

Relationship behavior is the way in which the supervisor attends to the follower at the personal level. When relationship behavior is high (strong), the supervisor listens, provides support and involves the follower in decision-making.

The two dimensions can be combined, using only high or low levels of each, into four "styles" of leader behavior. These are illustrated in Figure 13.5.

The *hand-holding* style would sound something like this: "I have a job for you to do. Here are the details (leader outlines task details). It must be done by three o'clock today. I want you to do it this way (tells follower specifically how to do the work). I'll check back in a little while, but if you run into a snag, let me know immediately, so I can help you."

The *influence* style sounds exactly like the hand-holding style, up to a point. Here it is: "I have a job for you to do. Here are the details (leader outlines task details). It must be done by three o'clock today. I want you to do it this way (tells follower specifically how to do the work). [Here it changes.] The reason I want you to

Figure 13.5

My Model of Leadership

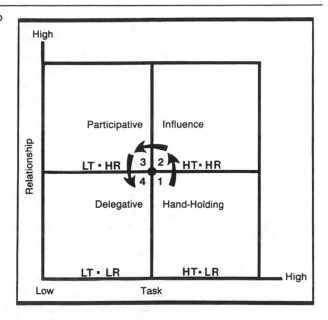

do it this way is (explains rationale for procedure). I'm sure you'll do a good job. I'll check back in a little while, but if you run into a snag, let me know immediately, so I can help you."

The *participative* style sounds like this: "I have a job for you. Here's what it's all about (describes the job). Let's kick around some ideas about how to do it. What do you think?

Finally, *delegative* sounds like this in the extreme case: "I have a job for you. Here it is. Do you need anything from me? Any questions? Great! Drive on!"

The style which is best depends on the nature of the situation, which is a combination of the follower's skills and the difficulty of the job to be done.

Note that the proper style depends on how you answer the questions:

> **Can** the person do the job?
>> and
> **Will** the person take responsibility for doing it?

The dimensions of *can* and *will* combine to yield what might be called the person's *job maturity.* If the person's job maturity is very low, you need to do a lot of hand-holding. On the other hand, a high-maturity follower can be delegated to.

By combining the *can* and *will* answers, the appropriate style to use can be determined using the following guide:

Hand-holding:	Follower is unable and unwilling or insecure.
Influence:	Follower is unable but willing to do the job.
Participative:	Follower is able but unwilling or lacks confidence.
Delegative:	Follower is both able and willing.

Following this model, an interesting point can be made. As an employee's job maturity increases, the supervisor can eventually delegate to him. This frees the supervisor to attend to other matters. For that reason, it is clear that delegative management would be the ideal style, despite the strong advocacy for participative management. However, it is difficult to get all employees into quadrant four, so participative style is probably a good "average."

Nevertheless, part of a leader's responsibility is to develop people over time so that they are moved from quadrant 1 to 2, then to 3, and finally to 4. At that point, the follower can be promoted or given more responsibility. This will cause his or her job maturity to drop, so that a quadrant 2 or 3 style will have to be adopted, until the person is pulled back into quadrant 4, where the process starts again.

Over time, leaders continue to "slide" followers back and forth through the quadrants until the follower arrives at the same competence level as the leader. (Hopefully, by the time that happens, the leader will have advanced, since his or her boss should be applying the same model to the leader.)

Of course, not all people want to advance beyond a certain level, so for them, this process cannot continue indefinitely. Note also, that if an employee is promoted "too far-too fast," then that person may become a victim of the Peter Principle, which says, "Employees eventually rise to their level of incompetence."[12]

It is up to managers to see that employees are not promoted to a level of incompetence and then just left there. If a person is put into a position that is over his or her head, then the supervisor should begin pulling that person back up or remove him or her from that position.

In a project environment, this model can be used by a manager to decide just how much freedom members of a project team can be given. If they work for a functional manager, then that person should be practicing this model. However, if they do not know the model, the project manager can explain it and suggest to the functional manager how the person should be supervised.

If a very inexperienced person is assigned to the project and his or her supervisor does not provide handholding supervision, the project manager would have cause for alarm, and should discuss his or her concerns with that functional manager. If the manager is the kind of person who prefers to loosely supervise everyone, then the project manager might have to request that a more experienced person be assigned, or if possible, supervise the person himself.

Whatever the case, the model provides a practical way of deciding how to supervise people and emphasizes that no single style is adequate.

Key Points

- A leader must practice vision, involvement and persistence.

- People tend to behave in the way that you expect, so it pays to have high expectations for them.

- There is no single best style of supervising people—it depends on their job maturity.

- You cannot talk one line and behave in a contrary way. People will lose respect for you.

CHAPTER 14 How to Motivate *Almost* Anyone

When Imhotep built the great step pyramid, he probably didn't have to worry much about motivating the people who worked on it. Many of them were slaves. Their motivation was to stay alive.

However, that does not explain the accomplishments of hundreds of other project leaders who built astonishing monuments which inspire awe in us today. Through the centuries, they have been able to coordinate the efforts of thousands of people to build the henges in the British Isles, the beautiful temples of the Mayans, and others too numerous to mention. How did these project leaders motivate the people to do back-breaking work without using threats of punishment or death or the great carrot of today—money?

In my ten years of teaching seminars throughout the United States, Canada and San Juan, the most frequently asked question is undoubtedly, "How do you motivate people?" There seems to be almost universal concern that people are not motivated to perform those jobs that need to be done in the workplace. The consensus among managers seems to be that the only reason many people come to work is to get a paycheck. They have a somewhat Theory-X outlook, to use McGregor's terminology.

I have concluded from conversations with thousands of people that, in many cases, what they really mean is, "How do we get people to want to do jobs that no one in their right mind would want to do?" When it comes to motivation, I'm afraid we have some very unrealistic attitudes. Perhaps it is because we don't really understand what motivation is all about. (See Figure 14.1.)

In several of my classes, there have been individuals who engage in cliff climbing as a sport. In one class, someone asked a cliff climber, "What do you think about when you're up there on that cliff?"

"Do you really want to know?" he asked.

"Yes."

"I'm thinking, 'If I ever get off this thing, I'll never do this again!'"

"Really!?"

"Yes. Really!"

The questioner looked puzzled. "Then I don't understand. Why do you do it again?"

The cliff climber thought for a moment, then said, "I don't know. Maybe I'm crazy, but someone tells me about another cliff somewhere that is a real challenge, and I can't wait to see if I can do it."

This example strikes me as demonstrating the essence of what we mean by motivation. The cliff climber has a built-in drive to engage in his sport, and all you have to do is tell him about a cliff that is a challenge, and he can't wait to try it. No one has to pay him. He doesn't have to be begged, threatened, or persuaded. He does it because of a drive from within himself. And that is what motivation is all about.

Figure 14.1

How to Get People
Started

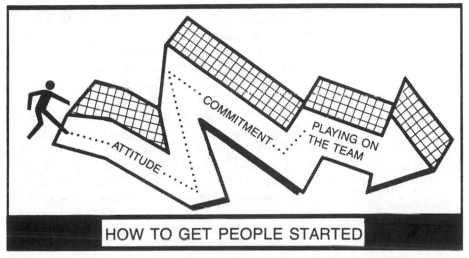

True motivation comes from within the individual.
We call such motivation *intrinsic*. Any attempt to get
someone to want to do something by offering him or her
external rewards is an effort to use *extrinsic* motivation.

In my own case, I have no intrinsic drive to climb
cliffs. I have vertigo. If I get ten feet off the ground, I
get dizzy. For that reason, no one can arouse in me a desire to climb a sheer rock cliff.

"Suppose someone gave you a million dollars?" a
person asked me once. "Would that motivate you to do
it?"

My response was, "I might climb a cliff to get a million dollars, but I would not be motivated by the task
itself, and once I had finished it and collected my million dollars, I certainly would not likely want to do it
again."

This leads people to believe that you can motivate
someone with money. It is an argument that probably
goes back to the invention of money over 2500 years
ago, and it is a very heated argument. Those people who
are adamant that they themselves are motivated by
money miss a subtle point. It is not the money itself that

231

motivates, but all the things they know they can do with the money that "turns them on."

Money is a *symbol* for many things—power, security, prestige, status, comfort, and all the other things that humans desire. So when you offer someone a lot of money to do something, they may perform admirably because they are thinking of what the money represents—or of what they can do with it. The interesting thing is, if they were not paid again to perform that same task, they probably never would.

The cliff climber, on the other hand, continues to climb cliffs, even though no one pays him to do so. What we should learn from this is that *intrinsic* motivation is durable. *Extrinsic* motivation exists only so long as the external rewards are available. As soon as they are withdrawn, the individual no longer cares to perform the task.

In my opinion, the real conclusion to be drawn from this is that the only *real* motivation is intrinsic. The term extrinsic, while it is used by psychologists and other professional students of motivation, is a misnomer. For that reason, we need to adopt a realistic approach to motivation in organizations and use intrinsic factors as much as possible.

This is contrary to majority practice, and I believe it is the reason why organizations have so much difficulty with motivation. They have relied almost exclusively on extrinsic factors to motivate people and failed to take advantage of intrinsic factors.

What this means is that we would try to place people in jobs which they would find intrinsically motivating, rather than giving them a job that is boring, unchallenging or mindless, and then trying to get them turned on to it by using externals.

Another point that seems to be overlooked is that we all must do some things that virtually no one wants to do. Around our homes, for example, the toilet must be cleaned, the house must be painted and the grass must be cut; for some people, those chores are no fun at all. Yet they do them because they are necessary. (As someone once told me, the alternatives are unacceptable!)

The thing is, we all know that, while we do those tasks—such as cleaning the toilet—we are not turned on to the task, but are looking forward to finishing it, so we can do something that we really enjoy.

The same thing is true of organizations. There are, figuratively speaking, toilet-cleaning jobs at work. What we must realize is that, while someone must do those jobs, we cannot expect them to be turned on to the task, and it is senseless to beat our heads against the wall trying to find a way to motivate the person to clean toilets.

What we should do is to distribute the toilet-cleaning jobs as evenly as possible, so no one person gets stuck having to do them all the time, and we should attempt to eliminate as many of them as possible.

Given that we do this, the question still remains, "How do you know what kind of work will be intrinsically motivating to a person?" and this is *the* legitimate question we should ask. If we can answer this question for most of the people who work for us—and apply it— then most of the problems with motivation in the work place will be solved, and the remainder will not be of so much concern.

There are two theoretical models which have been taught for over thirty years in an attempt to help managers find out how to motivate people. One is Maslow's Need Hierarchy and the other is Herzberg's Motivation-Hygiene factors. Both have merits, but managers who have attempted to apply them have often had limited success.

What is needed is a method of finding out for each individual what motivates him or her, and that is something that the models do not deliver. Such a technique has been devised, and will be presented later in this chapter. First, however, it is useful to know what Maslow and Herzberg said about motivation, because they provide a conceptual base from which to work.

Maslow's Hierarchy

Human beings have a large number of needs. When those needs are active, we are motivated to satisfy them. Abraham Maslow suggested that human needs can be grouped into five general categories, which vary in strength, depending on whether they have been recently satisfied. He arranged those needs in a hierarchy, because he believed that the category at the bottom of the hierarchy (the lower-level needs) must be satisfied before the upper-level needs emerge. His hierarchy is shown in Figure 14.2

The terms have the following meanings:

Self-actualization: The need to be everything one is capable of being. Self-mastery.

Esteem: The need to be thought well of by significant others.

Social: The need to affiliate with other people.

Safety: The need to provide for unexpected happenings and to feel secure from harm.

Physiological: The biological needs, including hunger, warmth, sex, shelter, etc.

Maslow suggested that the lower three levels of his hierarchy are basic maintenance needs. The individual must have these needs met in order to experience well-being. The top two levels are those that are important in bringing about valued organizational performance. The manager's job, according to the theory, is to help individuals satisfy those basic maintenance needs so that the needs for recognition (or esteem) and self-actualization will become active.

In my experience, this is easier to say than to do. It is very difficult to know exactly where in the hierarchy an individual falls and how to help him or her satisfy basic maintenance needs.

Furthermore, there is very little research evidence that supports Maslow's theory that needs are arranged in a hierarchy. Of course, Maslow suggested that all levels of the hierarchy can be active at once, rather than progressing in an all-or-nothing manner. That is, physiological needs do not have to be satisfied completely before higher-level needs emerge. However, it seems intuitively correct to say that a starving person will not be too concerned about higher-level needs until his or her hunger has been satisfied.

Figure 14.2

Maslow's Hierarchy

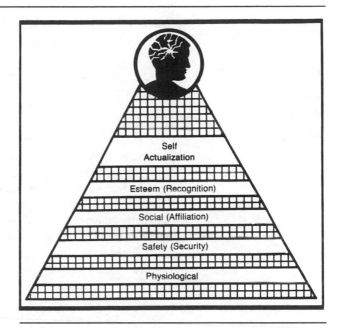

Self
Actualization

Esteem (Recognition)

Social (Affiliation)

Safety (Security)

Physiological

Nevertheless, counter-examples of the hierarchy can be found. The "starving artist" is self-actualizing, despite the fact that her lower-level needs may not be met. She is so totally consumed by the drive to express herself through her art that she suppresses the lower-level needs.

Many examples serve as guides to how people are actually motivated. Many people disprove the hierarchy by their actions: The athlete who submits to grueling training exercises in pursuit of excellence in his sport. The engineer who spends long hours struggling to solve some very difficult technical problem. Likewise, the entrepreneur who works seven days a week for long periods to build a business disproves the idea that lower-level needs must be satisfied first.

Such examples actually suggest that when people give themselves totally to something that for them is a way of fully expressing themselves (self-actualizing), they are not very concerned about the lower needs. Again, this suggests that we must change our approach to motivation in the work place. If we can somehow help the individual become self-actualizing, then the lower-level needs become less important.

Herzberg's Motivation—Hygiene Factors

Another model of motivation which has gained widespread attention is Herzberg's motivation-hygiene theory. Unlike Maslow's model, which was largely based on theoretical construction, Herzberg's model was derived from empirical research.

Herzberg conducted a number of field studies in which he asked workers to tell what things in their jobs "turned them on" and what things "turned them off." From an extensive analysis of the data, Herzberg concluded that the elements affecting motivation could be boiled down to a limited number of general factors. He called those factors that turn people off *hygiene* or *maintenance* factors, and he called the others *motivator* factors. These are shown in Table 14.1.

The hygiene factors, according to Herzberg, will turn people off to their jobs if they are not satisfied, but if they *are* satisfied, they do very little to motivate the person. That is, if they are satisfactory, they are neutral in terms of motivation, but if they are unsatisfactory, they are negative, or demotivators.

The application of Herzberg's model must take into account a human characteristic that is well understood at the personal level, but seems to be poorly comprehended in work situations. The principle is that, when people are in pain, their pain takes precedence over pleasure. We all know how debilitating a severe headache can be. It is difficult to enjoy activities which would ordinarily be very pleasurable when one has a bad headache.

In other words, a person cannot be "turned on" and "turned off" at the same time, and being turned off takes priority. Stated in more formal terms, a person cannot experience two opposite emotions simultaneously.

Given that this is true, Herzberg said that we must take care of the hygiene factors first, before we attempt to apply the motivators. That is, if the hygiene factors in an organization are unsatisfactory, they will cause peo-

Table 14.1

Herzberg's Motivation
and Hygiene

Motivation Factors	Hygiene Factors
Achievement	Company policy and ad-
Recognition	ministration
Work itself	Supervision
Responsibility	Relationship with supervisor
Advancement	Work conditions
Growth	Salary
	Relationships with peers
	Personal life
	Relationships with subordi-
	nates
	Status
	Security

ple to be demotivated, so they must be "cleaned up" before the motivators can be applied.

Of course, it is not an all-or-nothing proposition. The hygiene factors can be a bit unsatisfactory and a person can still be motivated, but if the degree of "discomfort" becomes very high, then motivation will suffer.

However, in some organizations, the hygiene factors are so greatly out-of-line for so many employees that, if they were taken care of, those organizations would probably find that they actually have very little problem with motivation. Indeed, it is my belief that this is true for most organizations.

For example, the first item listed under hygiene factors is company policy. This is one of the most common offenders, in my experience. As Tom Peters has argued in his book, *Thriving On Chaos,* organizations have so many "Mickey Mouse" policies that it is no wonder employees are disgruntled.

Many companies have a policy that establishes a spending limit on employees.[1] The limit goes up as the level of the employee increases, but there is always a limit. There is no quarrel with such a policy in general. The quarrel is with the *level* of the limit.

Tom Peters tells about one newly hired engineering director who discovered that his engineers had a $25 limit. Anything which they wanted to buy for more than $25 had to be approved by someone higher in the organization. He raised the level to $200. The accounting department screamed bloody murder. "Those people will take us to the cleaners," they claimed. "You have no control over spending now." The result? Spending dropped 60 percent.

The reason? The engineers were so insulted at being treated like children (as they saw it) that they were playing "stick-it-to-them." Their response was, let's see how many $24.99 things we can buy—they don't have to be approved.

It might be argued that such action proves the validity of the policy. They were behaving irresponsibly. The evidence does not warrant that conclusion, however. As soon as they were treated as though they were responsible, they began to behave that way.

It is my feeling that most policies represent a "cop-out" on the part of management. Because a few employees behave badly, the organization makes a policy which is intended to limit the behavior of all employees. They do this, rather than deal one-on-one with the offenders, and thereby lose the loyalty and commitment of "good" employees.

Among the hygiene factors, the word "relationship" occurs several times. When employees are in relationships at work which are disagreeable, they are turned off, and one of the most important of those is the relationship with the supervisor. This is why supervisors—in this case, project managers—must work to maintain good relationships with team members.

This does not mean that the manager must run a popularity contest, or that all relationships will be of a highly friendly nature. It does mean that all relationships must be built on mutual respect. Where this is not possible, the employee should be transferred to another supervisor (if possible), both for the benefit of the employee and the supervisor with whom the bad relationship exists.

In support of what was said at the beginning of this chapter about salary, Herzberg found that for eighty to ninety percent of his respondents, pay is a hygiene factor. That is, if pay is satisfactory, it is neutral in terms of motivation, but if it is unsatisfactory, it is negative.

There are two components to determine whether pay is satisfactory. First, is it in line with what one's peers are making? Women in our society are sometimes victims of this. Why should a man make more for doing the same job than a woman?

Second, is the person's pay adequate to meet his or her needs? If not, then he or she will be dissatisfied and will take steps to correct for the problem. That often means leaving the job, as it is sometimes impossible to get a larger salary.

Pay can serve as an extrinsic source of motivation when there is a direct correlation between performance and pay. That is the intention of piece-rate and commission sales jobs, and indeed, people will usually work harder under those conditions to make more money. Unfortunately, numerous stories are told about companies that change the pay or commission scale to keep employees from making more than some maximum level, thereby creating resentment and destroying any incentive to work.

The other factors in the list are fairly straightforward. When people are made to feel like low-status individuals (by treating them as if they are not important, for example), when they feel that their job security is threatened (by automation, among other things), or when working conditions are bad, they will be demotivated.

To sum up Herzberg's "prescription," problems with the hygiene factors should be corrected before an attempt is made to apply the motivators. The problem is, most project managers have limited control over these factors. Still, that does not mean *zero* control, and every manager should do whatever is possible to correct for any hygiene factors that are a problem. If direct control is not possible, one can at least lobby with higher-level managers to have them corrected.

Assuming that the hygiene factors have been taken care of, the motivators can be applied. These are all intangibles, and correspond roughly to the top two levels of Maslow's hierarchy, as shown in Figure 14.3. The problem, however, is still the same. How do you determine which of these factors will motivate a specific individual?

What About Unresponsive Al?

What indeed? What do you do about Al, who does not respond when you take care of the hygiene factors and try to challenge him? What about Al, who seems to have less drive than a snail? "How do I motivate him?" you ask.

Well, before you go too far, you need to answer a basic question, which is, "Is it worth the effort?"

"Gee, isn't that a bit callous?" you may ask. No. We are too easily trapped into trying to "save" employees who cannot and should not be saved. In my opinion, the most respectful and kindest way to deal with another person is to expect of him the best that he can do.

If he chooses not to respond to that expectation, which I cannot force on him, I can move him into a job that suits him or remove him from my organization if I have no such match. To keep someone in a slot for which he has no skills or incentive to perform is unfair to the person and to all other employees who are performing adequately.

There are two questions which must be answered before attempting to motivate Al:

- Does Al have the *potential* to perform adequately in the job?
- Does Al *want* to perform adequately in the job?

Unless you can answer "yes" to both questions, then you should consider transferring Al to another job or terminating his employment.

Motivation Patterns: A New Model of Motivation

Suppose you decide that Al has potential and wants to do a good job, but for some reason the job doesn't challenge him. How can you determine what *would* challenge him?

You could ask him, but many people can't tell you. They have never really thought about it. For others, they don't want to tell you—for any number of reasons.

Figure 14.3

Maslow and Herzberg
Compared

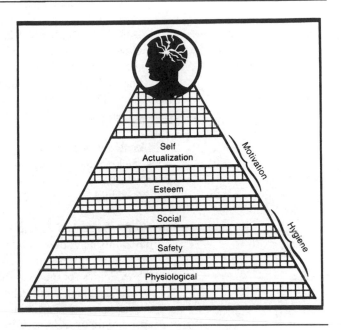

You could try giving Al a lot of different assignments, until you find one that turns him on, but that
consumes a lot of time, which is something you don't
have much of in a project environment. You need a
method of finding out what motivates Al which can be
done fairly quickly and which gives an accurate answer.

Such a method does exist, and I have used it
throughout the United States with several thousand people, and have found only a very small number (less than
a dozen) for whom the method didn't work. Here are examples of the questions I ask:

- Tell me about some job you've had, during the past
  six months to a year, which you really enjoyed. You
  looked forward to working on it, put a lot of yourself into it, perhaps thought about it on the way to
  work, considering what you were going to do about
  some particular aspect of the job. I don't need to
  know a lot of heavy technical detail, but I want to

know the part you played in the job, what you feel you contributed to it, and so on.

CAUTION: Don't say, "Tell me about your present job and what you like about it." The person may currently be in a job that is demotivating.

If he can't think of any job he has had during that time frame, I ask him to think back over his entire career and tell me about the one job that stands out in his mind.

As he tells me about the job, I pay very close attention—make notes if necessary, and probe for additional information.

Next, I ask:

- Now let me ask if you have some hobbies, sports, or other outside interests that you like to spend time with. If he tells me no, I go back and ask for more job examples (or move to the final question which I will present later). When he says he does have some outside interests, I ask him to pick one that he would spend more time doing if he had it.

The pitfall here is that someone will tell you he likes to jog, which he does because he thinks he should for health reasons, but he wouldn't spend more time doing it if the time were made available. Such activities are not motivators as such, so I avoid them, and ask the person to give me another example.

Finally, I say:

- Now tell me—is there anything you've always wanted to do but never got to do—maybe because you didn't have the time or money, or your family responsibilities prevented it? Call it a fantasy or wish list if you like. Is there anything like that? If so, tell me about it.

These questions can be used as presented, or if the person cannot relate to one of them, you can use the other two. In other words, I could use jobs, hobbies, or wish-lists alone or in any combination, so long as I have at least three examples of something that motivates the person.

Now what you do is look for the common thread or pattern that runs through the three motivators, and the important thing here is that it is the *pattern of activity* that is the motivator, not the content of the activity, per se. People achieve self-actualization through engaging in a repetitive pattern of activity. Once you have determined that pattern of activity, you can then try to give the person assignments which contain that pattern.

As an example, some people are motivated by a pattern of activity which can be described as the *trouble-shooter* pattern. They love to fix things. Give them a broken *anything* (within reason, of course) and they are driven to repair it.

Another pattern is the *innovator*. The person who is an innovator is always trying to come up with something new. Thomas Edison undoubtedly was motivated by innovation.

There is also the *helper*. Many helpers are found in education, nursing, counseling, and volunteer positions. They are turned on by being able to be helpful to others.

Michael Maccoby, in his book *Why Work?* lists five "types" of people, including the innovator and helper. In addition, he has the Expert, Defender, and Self-Developer. Most individuals combine two or more of these, but usually one will be dominant.

Maccoby lists only five types, however, and there are definitely more than that. He does not list the troubleshooter, for example. By using the method presented above, you can find a person's pattern no matter what it is and whether it fits Maccoby's types or not.

In fact, I prefer not to create too many labels for patterns. There is a temptation to "pigeon-hole" people into categories and miss important characteristics which do not fit a particular mold. For that reason, I encourage people to stay open to whatever information the person offers and determine the pattern without attempting to label it.

It is also important to note that nearly everyone likes a challenge of some kind. However, what is a challenge for one would not be a challenge for another. The challenge of cliff-climbing would be sheer terror for me, for example. So before you conclude glibly that the person likes a challenge, you must be able to say what that means for that particular individual.

Once you know the pattern of activity that motivates a person, you can then try to assign work that will contain that pattern. If you have no such jobs, that is useful to know, because you now know why he has been unmotivated by his or her current position.

If this is the case, then a transfer or termination are possible. Or—and this is always an option—you may decide that you can live with the person's level of performance. I don't recommend this very often, but there are circumstances that might justify it, such as when the individual has only another year or so until retirement, an has been with the company twenty-five years and in the past was an acceptable worker. For most people, however, I still prefer to see them work at full capacity (which is a value judgment on my part).

In order to learn this method, I have devised an exercise which I use in my seminars. You can also do it yourself, if you follow the instructions. (See Table 14.2.) I suggest that you do this with two other people; otherwise, you have to do everything yourself. It takes some practice to become comfortable with the questioning method, and also to learn to find the pattern that runs through the three examples. By practicing with two other people, you will feel more comfortable when you apply it to an employee.

CAUTION: Be careful not to "lead" the subject too much, or you will get *your* motivation pattern and not his or hers.

Table 14.2

Exercise: Eliciting
Motivation Patterns

1. Get into groups of three people each. One person will be the interviewer, one the subject, and one the observer/time keeper. In class, you should limit yourselves to about fifteen minutes to get information from the subject and process it.

2. The interviewer asks the subject the questions outlined in the text above. The observer should pay close attention, so he or she can help the interviewer process that information when the interview is completed.

3. After all information has been obtained, the interviewer and observer should put your heads together and see if you can find the pattern. Make sure it seems right to the subject. If he or she objects, look more closely. You probably missed something.

4. Now rotate, twice, so that all three of you "play" all three roles.

Key Points

- Real motivation is internal to the person, and is called *intrinsic.* Extrinsic motivation is an attempt to use rewards such as money or recognition to give the person incentive to do something.

- Motivation is the arousal of built-in drives. If a drive does not exist, there is nothing to arouse.

- Maslow grouped human needs into five categories and arranged them in a hierarchy, and said that the lower-level needs must be satisfied in order for the upper-level needs to emerge.

- Herzberg called hygiene factors those aspects of the work situation which are neutral if they are satisfactory, but which turn people off if they are not okay.

- The hygiene factors should be taken care of first, since a person cannot be turned on and turned off at the same time.

- A person achieves self-actualization by engaging in a repetitive pattern of activity. Once that pattern is known, the person can be given job assignments that contain the pattern.

Section Seven

A Sample Project Plan

CHAPTER 15 Developing a Sample Project Plan

In order to illustrate the principles presented in this book, it is necessary to choose a sample project that a person from any discipline can follow. That in itself is a tall order, but I have found one that fits the requirements fairly well.

The sample project presented is to develop a training program for new project managers. A general description follows. The example includes most of the core elements from the list of contents recommended for a project plan. Not included are a SWOT analysis, contractual requirements or a control system.

General Description

This training program will be offered by Lewis Consulting & Training on both a public and in-company basis. That is, public programs will be offered, which can be attended by anyone, and the class will also be offered to companies that have enough trainees to make their own class, usually in the range of ten to thirty participants.

The class includes a participant workbook, some overhead transparencies and a number of exercises to help participants develop their competence in applying the skills being taught. Following are the components of the plan together with commentary on various elements.

The Project Plan

The first step is to develop a problem statement:

Problem Statement

New project managers usually have no formal training in the tools and techniques of project management. They do not know how to plan, schedule or control a project, and therefore try to manage by the "seat-of-the-pants."

Based on this problem statement, an overall statement of the goal of the project can be written:

Project Goal

By August 30, 1991, develop a training program to teach new project managers how to plan, schedule, and control a project.

Next, a statement of the scope of the project might be written.

Project Scope

The training program will include the essential tools of project management, including how to plan, how to schedule using either CPM or PERT methods, how to allocate resources in scheduling and how to do variance or earned-value analysis. It will not include training in supervisory skills, as these are already available in another course. The course is also not aimed at experienced project managers, and so no advanced concepts will be presented.

A mission statement for this project will not be developed. However, a general statement of the approach to be followed is in order. Likewise, a few of the objectives of the project are also needed.

Approach

The workbook will be prepared by the instructor, using word-processing combined with clip art and conventional illustrations. Desktop publishing will not be used. The camera-ready art will be provided to a printer for preparation of workbooks. Overhead transparencies to support the text will be prepared as required. The workbook will contain ample space for participants to take notes.

Objectives

Following are a few objectives of the project.

1. To present a program which will enable a learner to put together a plan, schedule, and control system by the end of the class.
2. To develop a course that is highly practical, rather than theoretical. (No date is needed for this objective.)
3. To have the course reviewed by at least two experienced project managers by September 30, 1991.

Deliverables

A list of deliverables would include the following: A workbook to be used in the class; overhead transparencies to illustrate significant points covered in the class; handouts to be used in testing a learner's understanding of the material and for use in class exercises; structured exercises to illustrate the development of a WBS, the development of a CPM schedule (no resource allocation involved) and the interpretation of a progress report using variance measures.

Specifications

Specifications for a training program might be in the form of an outline.

The course content will conform to the outline attached. (The outline is not included in this sample plan.)

The Work Breakdown Structure

At this point, the planner could prepare a WBS for the project as illustrated by Figure 15.1.

The WBS involves three tasks: (1) the program content must be determined, (2) the class workbook must be

Figure 15.1

Work Breakdown
Structure for Sample
Project

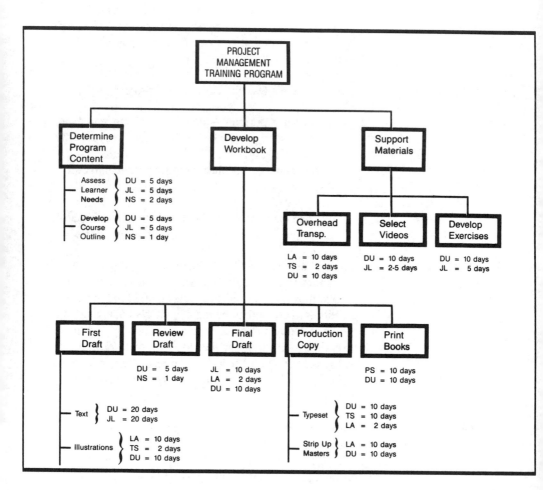

developed, and (3) the supporting materials must be developed. The work needed for each task are subtasks; for simplicity, they will be referred to as *activities* in this chapter.

For each activity, the duration is shown in days, together with the initials of the resource(s) to be applied and their working times in days. Durations are coded as *DU* in the figure.

Preliminary Arrow Diagram

When this has been completed, a schedule can be prepared. Project Workbench was used to develop the schedules which follow. However, it is always a good idea to draw an arrow diagram of a schedule before entering data into the computer, since the precedence relationships will have to be entered and are difficult to work out on the screen. For that reason, an arrow diagram was first drawn as shown in Figure 15.2.

This is a fairly simple arrow diagram. It is drawn with the critical path running straight down the center, which is conventional. The diagram is an activity-on-arrow network, and the events show the early and late times in working days.

The logic shown indicates that the illustrations for the text can be drawn beginning after the first draft has been completed. The selection of supporting videos could also be made at that time. Both tasks have a generous amount of float. The illustrations will be stripped into the typeset pages to form camera-ready copy to be used in printing the books, so that arrow comes back in before the strip-up activity begins.

Overheads are not done until final typesetting is complete. It might be argued that they should not be done until pages are stripped up, since they may simply be copies of workbook pages. In that case, two critical paths would exist, since print books would be in parallel with the overheads. This would be acceptable. It is also possible to overlap the overheads with the strip-up activity. That is, as soon as some of the pages have been stripped up, the overheads could be made from them.

It is also possible, however, that the overheads are being designed to stand alone. That is more-or-less how I viewed it and is why I drew the diagram as shown. I

Figure 15.2

Arrow Diagram for Project

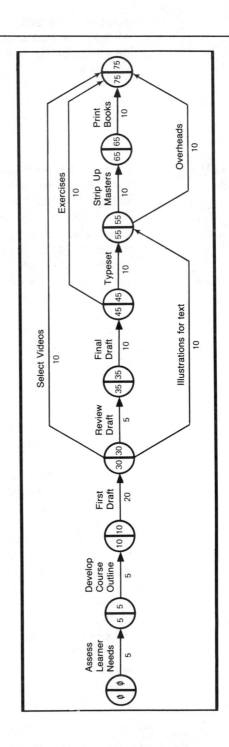

did consider that some of the material already developed might be used, so I held the overheads until this point in time for that reason.

The exercises to be used in giving participants practice with the course content can be designed only after the final draft. This activity has a lot of float, since it is in parallel with three ten-day activities.

The Initial Schedule

Figure 15.3 contains the Gantt chart for the project, as determined by standard CPM computation, that is, assuming unlimited resources. As the resource levels underneath the schedule show, overloads occur for Jim & Lea Ann Lewis and for Norman Smith at the highlighted points. At the left side of the resource summary, the column headed *Day* shows the availability of each resource on a weekly basis. Except for Norman Smith, all resources are available five days each week. His availability, however, is only one day each week. That is, he is available only on a part-time basis.

There are holidays shown at two points in the schedule. One holiday is the week of July 4th. Note the letter *H* which appears at the top of the printout, beginning at July 1, and a single *H* at September 2, which is the Labor Day holiday in 1991. These holidays cause the schedule to be extended by six days beyond what would be possible in strict working time.

As shown, the schedule could end on October 8, 1991. However, this cannot happen unless the resource overloads are corrected. This might be done by working overtime, but at this point, we do not know if that is necessary.

When CPM computations are made, all activities are scheduled to start at the earliest possible time, reserving activity float to be used only if necessary. It might be possible to use some of that float to resolve the resource overloading.

To determine what the schedule would look like if resources were not overloaded, the *Autoschedule* routine of Workbench was run, using the contour loading heuristic, and all activity durations were treated as fixed. The solution shown in Figure 15.4 was obtained.

Figure 15.3

Gantt Chart, Unleveled

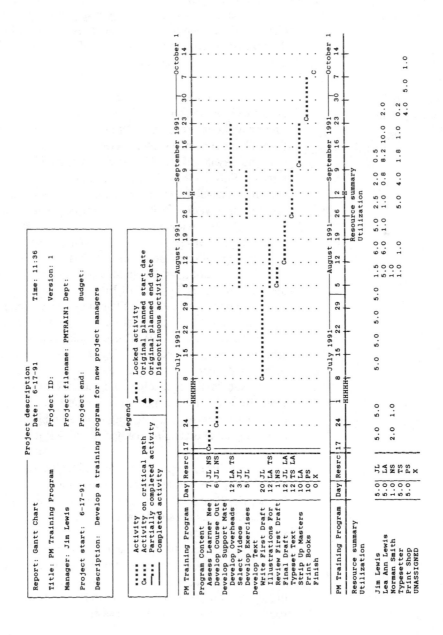

Figure 15.4

Gantt Chart,
Autoscheduled

```
------------------------------ Project description ------------------------------
| Report: Gantt Chart            Date:  6-17-91            Time: 14:45          |
|                                                                              |
| Title: PM Training Program     Project ID:               Version: 1          |
|                                                                              |
| Manager: Jim Lewis             Project filename: PMTRAIN1 Dept:              |
|                                                                              |
| Project start:  6-17-91        Project end:              Budget:             |
|                                                                              |
| Description:  Develop a training program for new project managers            |
------------------------------------------------------------------------------
```

```
------------------------------------- Legend ------------------------------------
|  .....  Activity                       ◆        Milestone                     |
|  C....  Activity on critical path      L....    Locked activity               |
|  ----.  Partially completed activity   -----    Completed activity            |
|  ▲      Original start date            ▼        Original end date             |
|  .....  Discontinuous activity         .....◆   Baselined milestone           |
---------------------------------------------------------------------------------
```

Gantt chart with PM Training Program activities and Resource summary.

The overload for Norman Smith still exists, because the activity to which he is applied is a single Critical Path activity, and the only way to resolve that problem is to increase his availability or reduce his required workload.

This solution shows what often happens in projects when resource limitations are not considered. This would be a very real-world situation in my case because only my wife and I would be available to do the work, and without working eighty-hour weeks at some points, the program could not be completed in its shortest possible time.

Figure 15.5 contains a listing of the activities printed from Workbench. It shows the start and end dates for each activity, the duration in business days, the resources applied, their usage and the cost for each. As each resource is assigned to the project, a cost per day is entered, so that Workbench can calculate project costs. No cost per day was assigned to the print shop, since they would charge so much per book, rather than charging a labor cost. The total labor cost for the project, then, is shown as $38,400.

Next, in Figure 15.6 a printout shows the first and last dates in the project for which each resource is used, together with the daily rate for each, the two-letter code by which each is identified, and the total working-days used and the cost for that usage. Again, the total project cost is shown as $38,400.

Finally, Figure 15.7 shows the CPM diagram printed by Workbench. This is an activity-on-node diagram. As the legend shows, the date in the box is the start date for the activity, followed by its duration in working days and its float. Critical activities are surrounded by double lines, and the non-critical activities by single lines. Note the finish box. I put this in so Workbench would print a final box showing when the project ends. Actually, since Workbench will not accept a zero-duration task, the project would end on the previous day.

Schedule With Overlapping Work

As drawn in the original diagram, the project requires that the first draft be completed before it can be re-

Figure 15.5

Activity Listing

ACTIVITY DETAIL
PM Training Program
Original Dates and Usage

Name	Start	End	Duration Bus. days	Resource assignments Name	Usage	Cost
Program Content						
Assess Learner Needs	6-17-91	6-21-91	5	Jim Lewis	5.0	2,000
				Norman Smith	2.0	800
Develop Course Outline	6-24-91	6-28-91	5	Jim Lewis	5.0	2,000
				Norman Smith	1.0	400
Develop Support Materials						
Develop Overheads	10-08-91	10-21-91	10	Lea Ann Lewis	10.0	4,000
				Typesetter	2.0	600
Select Videos	8-05-91	8-16-91	10	Jim Lewis	2.5	1,000
Develop Exercises	8-26-91	9-09-91	10	Jim Lewis	5.0	2,000
Develop Text						
Write First Draft	7-08-91	8-02-91	20	Jim Lewis	20.0	8,000
Illustrations For Text	9-10-91	9-23-91	10	Lea Ann Lewis	10.0	4,000
				Typesetter	2.0	600
Review First Draft	8-05-91	8-09-91	5	Norman Smith	1.0	400
Final Draft	8-12-91	8-23-91	10	Jim Lewis	10.0	4,000
				Lea Ann Lewis	2.0	800
Typeset Text	8-26-91	9-09-91	10	Typesetter	10.0	3,000
				Lea Ann Lewis	2.0	800
Strip Up Masters	9-24-91	10-07-91	10	Lea Ann Lewis	10.0	4,000
Print Books	10-08-91	10-21-91	10	Print Shop	10.0	0
Finish	10-22-91	10-22-91	1	UNASSIGNED		0
Total project	6-17-91	10-22-91	86	Total days	109.5	
				Total cost		38,400

Figure 15.6

Resource Usage								PAGE
JUN 17 91			**ACTIVITY DETAIL**					**2**
			PM Training Program					
			Original Dates and Usage					
Name			Start	End	Duration	Resource assignments		
					Bus. days	Name	Usage	Cost
Resource summary								
Name	**Units**	**Amt.**						
Jim Lewis	days	400	6-17-91	9-09-91		JL	47.5	19,000
Lea Ann Lewis	days	400	8-12-91	10-21-91		LA	34.0	13,600
Norman Smith	days	400	6-17-91	8-09-91		NS	4.0	1,600
Typesetter	days	300	8-26,91	10-21-91		TS	14.0	4,200
Print Shop	days		10-08-91	10-21-91		PS	10.0	0
UNAS-SIGNED	days		10-22-91	10-22-91		X		0
Total project			6-17-91	10-22-91	86	Total days	109.5	
						Total cost		38,400

viewed. The same is true for the reviews. They must be completed before the final draft can be done. However, if the book were reviewed on a chapter-by-chapter basis, perhaps the project duration could be reduced.

This was discussed in Chapter Five as *overlapping* work. One example of such overlapping is the ladder network. Another was the use of activity splitting. Workbench permits overlapping or splitting to allow a project to be shortened.

Figure 15.8 contains a new arrow diagram showing how activities must be connected in order to do a CPM computation. The following tasks have been split into two segments:

Activity Description	Segment 1	Segment 2
First Draft	5	15
Reviews	4	1
Final Draft	2	8
Typesetting	2	8
Strip-up	2	8

The illustrations are also overlapped with the first draft, but must be completed before the strip-up activity, so that the arrow goes down one side of the ladder and

Figure 15.7

CPM Diagram

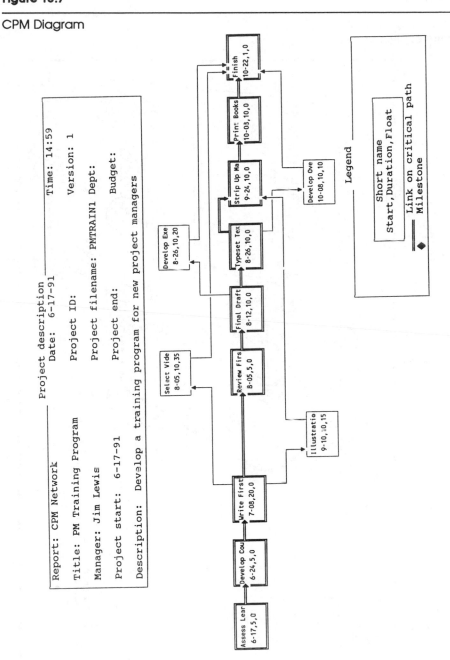

Figure 15.8

Arrow Diagram with
Activities Overlapped

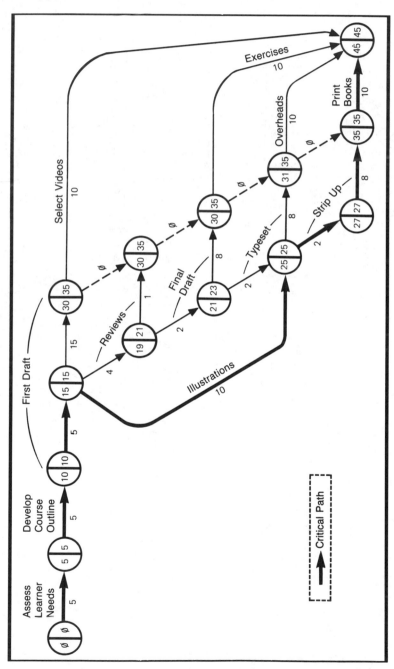

actually winds up on the critical path. Similarly, other parallel tasks come off at appropriate points and converge on the final event. The zero-duration dummies shown are necessary to correctly connect the activities logically. If the end points of the activities were allowed to hang out in "mid-air," so-to-speak, then they would be called "dangles," and an incorrect network computation would result.

The arrow diagram shows a possible completion time of forty-five days after start, ignoring any possible resource limitations. Figure 15.9 shows the Gantt chart for the schedule, and the resource loading underneath definitely shows some problems. Resource overloads have been highlighted. If the total working-days duration for the project is scaled off the Gantt chart, it turns out to be forty-five, verifying that Workbench does indeed arrive at the same conclusion as the manual calculation.

This solution certainly does yield a project completion well in advance of the one with no work overlapped. The original CPM scheduled end-date was October 8, whereas this one is August 26. That is a six-week gain on project completion.

However, unless resources are worked with heavy overtime, or unless more people can be put on the project to increase resource availability, the end-date is not realistic. For this reason, an autoschedule routine was run, to determine the realistic end-date. This solution is shown in Figure 15.10.

As the schedule shows, most of the overlaps are gone. The illustrations and reviews are overlapped with the first draft, and the typesetting is still overlapped with the final draft. The end-date is now September 19. This is still about two-and-one-half weeks earlier than the original CPM schedule yielded, thus offering a definite gain in throughput, but because of limited resources it is a far cry from the shortest possible schedule.

The CPM printout from Workbench is shown in Figure 15.11. It looks the same as the original diagram, except that the critical path now runs along the illustrations, as was shown in the arrow diagram in Figure 15.8.

The CPM printout does not capture the graphics involved in overlapping tasks.

Figure 15.12 contains an activity listing. Note that the only differences between this listing and the previous one are the floats for the activities and the activity start and finish dates. What is significant is that activities that had float under unlimited-resource conditions now have none.

Final Comments

This sample project illustrates the usefulness of scheduling software to solve the resource-allocation problem. Although the network is fairly simple and the total number of resources is limited, the problem is a realistic one. (I do it all the time in my training work.)

Further, it required only about one hour to enter this data into the computer and to test several "what-if" scenarios in order to determine which would be suitable. Ten years ago this would have been virtually impossible for most project manager, simply because the software did not exist, except in huge mainframe incarnations, and even those were not nearly as user-friendly as the current personal computer software.

It seems to me, as a personal observation, that any project manager who has access to a personal computer should be able to deal with project scheduling much more effectively than was true in the past. While I have illustrated the problem using a small-scale project, the available software is capable of handling much larger ones.

Note, however, that the software is just a tool, and no tool can correct for sloppy planning, bad estimating or negative factors outside the control of the manager. Nor will it help with "people problems" that plague managers. is still about two-and-one-half weeks earlier than the original CPM schedule yielded, thus offering a

What it will do is allow you to get the most out of your skills, and that is the purpose for which this book was written.

Figure 15.9

Overlapped Activities
Unleveled

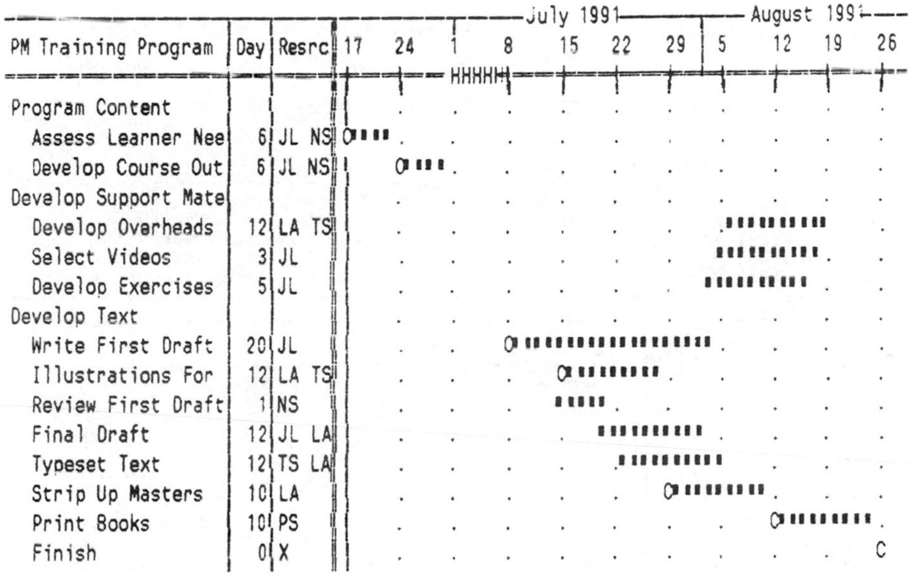

PM Training Program	Day	Resrc	17	24	1	8	15	22	29	5	12	19	26
						July 1991					August 1991		
Program Content													
Assess Learner Nee	6	JL NS	O▪▪▪	.		.	.		.		.		
Develop Course Out	6	JL NS		O▪▪▪	.		.		.		.		
Develop Support Mate				.		.	.		.		.		
Develop Overheads	12	LA TS		.		.	.		.		▪▪▪▪▪▪▪▪▪▪		
Select Videos	3	JL			.		.		.	▪▪▪▪▪▪▪▪▪▪	.		
Develop Exercises	5	JL			.		.		.	▪▪▪▪▪▪▪▪▪▪	.		
Develop Text					.		.		.		.		
Write First Draft	20	JL			.		O▪▪▪▪▪▪▪▪▪▪▪▪▪▪▪▪▪▪		.		.		
Illustrations For	12	LA TS			.		O▪▪▪▪▪▪▪▪▪		.		.		
Review First Draft	1	NS			.		▪▪▪▪▪	.		.		.		
Final Draft	12	JL LA			.		.	▪▪▪▪▪▪▪▪▪▪		.			
Typeset Text	12	TS LA			.		.	▪▪▪▪▪▪▪▪▪▪		.			
Strip Up Masters	10	LA			.		.		.	O▪▪▪▪▪▪▪▪	.		
Print Books	10	PS			.		.		.		O▪▪▪▪▪▪▪▪	.	
Finish	0	X			.		.		.		.		C

PM Training Program	Day	Resrc	17	24	1	8	15	22	29	5	12	19	26
						July 1991					August 1991		
Resource summary													
Utilization													
Jim Lewis	5.0	JL	5.0	5.0		5.0	6.0	10.0	9.5	4.0	3.0		
Lea Ann Lewis	5.0	LA					5.2	6.8	6.8	9.2	5.0	1.0	
Norman Smith	1.0	NS	1.0	1.0		1.0							
Typesetter	5.0	TS					1.0	5.0	5.0	1.8	1.0	0.2	
Print Shop	5.0	PS									5.0	5.0	
UNASSIGNED		X											

Figure 15.10

Overlapped Activities Autoscheduled

```
------------------------------ Project description -----------------------
| Report: Gantt Chart              Date:   6-17-91            Time: 13:28 |
| Title: PM Training Program       Project ID:               Version: 1  |
| Manager: Jim Lewis               Project filename: PMTRAIN2 Dept:       |
| Project start:  6-17-91          Project end:              Budget:      |
| Description:  Develop a training program for new project managers       |
------------------------------------------------------------------------
```

```
------------------------------ Legend -----------------------------------
| ·····   Activity                    ◆       Milestone                 |
| C····   Activity on critical path   L····   Locked activity           |
| -----   Partially completed activity -----  Completed activity        |
| ▲       Original start date         ▼       Original end date         |
| ·····   Discontinuous activity      ·····◆  Baselined milestone       |
------------------------------------------------------------------------
```

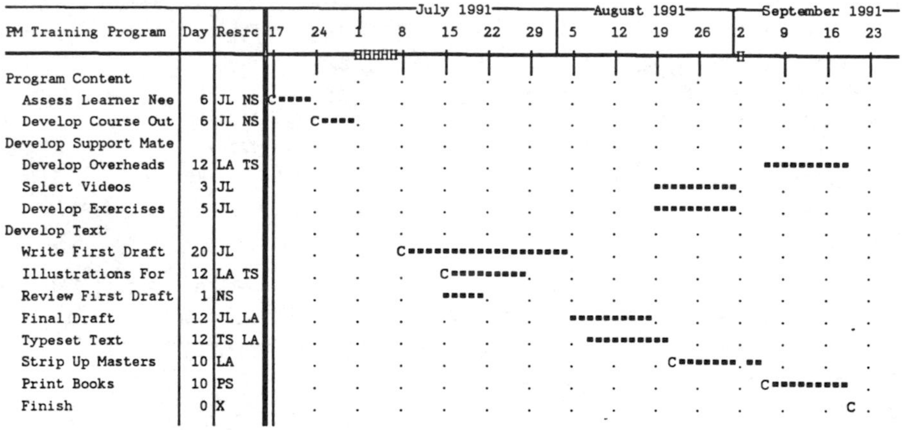

			July 1991				August 1991			September 1991	
PM Training Program	Day	Resrc	17	24	1 8	15	22	29	5	12 19 26	2	9 16 23
Program Content												
Assess Learner Nee	6	JL NS	C▪▪▪▪.									
Develop Course Out	6	JL NS	C▪▪▪▪.									
Develop Support Mate												
Develop Overheads	12	LA TS										▪▪▪▪▪▪▪▪▪▪ .
Select Videos	3	JL								▪▪▪▪▪▪▪▪▪▪		
Develop Exercises	5	JL								▪▪▪▪▪▪▪▪▪▪		
Develop Text												
Write First Draft	20	JL			C▪▪▪▪▪▪▪▪▪▪▪▪▪▪▪▪▪▪.							
Illustrations For	12	LA TS			C▪▪▪▪▪▪▪▪▪.							
Review First Draft	1	NS			▪▪▪▪▪.							
Final Draft	12	JL LA							▪▪▪▪▪▪▪▪▪▪			
Typeset Text	12	TS LA						▪	▪▪▪▪▪▪▪▪▪			
Strip Up Masters	10	LA								. C▪▪▪▪▪▪. ▪▪		
Print Books	10	PS									C▪▪▪▪▪▪▪▪.	
Finish	0	X										C .

			July 1991				August 1991			September 1991	
PM Training Program	Day	Resrc	17	24	1 8	15	22	29	5	12 19 26	2	9 16 23
Resource summary												
Utilization												
Jim Lewis	5.0	JL	5.0 5.0		5.0	5.0	5.0	5.0	5.0	5.0 4.0 3.5		
Lea Ann Lewis	5.0	LA				5.0	5.0		1.6	2.0 3.4 5.0	4.0	5.0 3.0
Norman Smith	1.0	NS	1.0 1.0		1.0							
Typesetter	5.0	TS				1.0	1.0		3.0	5.0 2.0	0.4	1.0 0.6
Print Shop	5.0	PS									2.0	5.0 3.0
UNASSIGNED		X										

Figure 15.11

CPM Diagram of
Overlapped Schedule

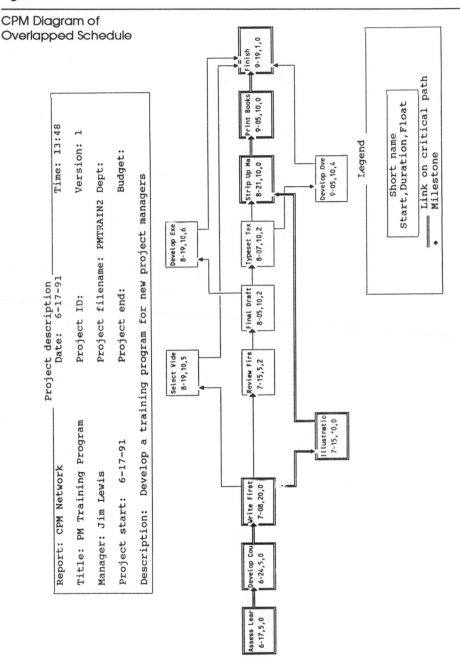

Figure 15.12

Activity Listing
Overlapped & Scheduled

JUN 17 91		ACTIVITY DETAIL				PAGE 1		
		PM Training Program						
		Original Dates and Usage						
Name	Start	End	Duration	Resource assignments				
			Bus Days	Name	Usage	Cost	Float	

Name	Start	End	Duration (Bus Days)	Resource Name	Usage	Cost	Float
Program Content							
Assess Learner							
Needs	6-17-91	6-21-91	5	Jim Lewis	5.0	2,000	0
				Norman Smith	1.0	400	
Develop Course							
Outline	6-24-91	6-28-91	5	Jim Lewis	5.0	2,000	0
				Norman Smith	1.0	400	
Develop Support Materials							
Develop							
Overheads	9-05-91	9-18-91	10	Lea Ann Lewis	10.0	4,000	4
				Typesetter	2.0	600	
Select Videos	8-19-91	8-30-91	10	Jim Lewis	2.5	1,000	5
Develop							
Exercises	8-19-91	8-30-91	10	Jim Lewis	5.0	2,000	6
Develop Text							
Write First Draft	7-08-91	8-02-91	20	Jim Lewis	20.0	8,000	0
Illustrations for							
Text	7-15-91	7-26-91	10	Lea Ann Lewis	10.0	4,000	0
				Typesetter	2.0	600	
Review First							
Draft	7-15-91	7-19-91	5	Norman Smith	1.0	400	2
Final Draft	8-05-91	8-16-91	10	Jim Lewis	10.0	4,000	2
				Lea Ann Lewis	2.0	800	
Typeset Text	8-07-91	8-20-91	10	Typesetter	10.0	3,000	2
				Lea Ann Lewis	2.0	800	
Strip Up							
Masters	9-21-91	9-04-91	10	Lea Ann Lewis	10.0	4,000	0
Print Books	9-05-91	9-18-91	10	Print Shop	10.0	0	0
Finish	9-19-91	9-19-91	1	UNASSIGNED		0	0
Total project	9-17-91	9-19-91	63	Total days	108.5		
				Total cost		38,000	

Checklist For Managing Projects

Instructions: Check each item to indicate that each activity has been completed. If the activity is not appropriate for this project, write N/A beside the item.

- A clear, concise statement defining the project has been prepared and reviewed by knowledgeable parties for consensus. ____

- Performance objectives have been written following guidelines in this book and each contains an actual *calendar date for completion.* ____

- A Work Breakdown Structure (WBS) has been developed to a level sufficient to prepare accurate estimates of costs, resources and working times for all project activities. ____

- A statement of project scope clearly defines the limits of what will and will not be done. _____

- Specifications that must be met are either identified or contained in the project notebook. _____

- Tangible deliverables have been identified for specific milestones to permit progress measurements. _____

- A Linear Responsibility Chart shows involvement of key contributors to the project. _____

- A working schedule has been prepared with adequate resources allocated so that significant planned overtime will not be required to meet project deadlines. _____

- A CPM or PERT diagram is the basis for all bar-chart working schedules, so that dependencies are known. _____

- A BCWS spending curve has been prepared to show cash flow throughout the project's duration. _____

- A SWOT analysis has been prepared, with particular attention to project risks. _____

- Where risks have been identified, contingency plans have been prepared to deal with them. _____

- If capital equipment is needed in the project, appropriate requisitions have been prepared, with cost justifications attached. _____

- The project plan has been prepared with participation and/or input from individuals who must implement it. _____

- The project notebook has been signed off by stakeholders, and copies distributed to contributors. _____

- A control system has been established using variance analysis to assess progress. _____

- All components of the project management system have been put in place, as defined by Figure 9.3. _____

- Individuals have been selected for assignment to the project; their needs will be met through active participation whenever possible. _____

- The project has been planned to a manageable level of detail. _____

- Work has been broken down into reasonable-duration tasks that are not likely to be back-end loaded. _____

- A post-mortem has been done at each milestone in the project as well as a final one for the overall project and placed in the project notebook. _____

- The controlling project notebook has been placed in a central file for use in future project planning. _____

- Members of the team have been instructed to record their working times on the project daily. _____

- A chart-of-accounts has been set up to track progress against the WBS. _____

- All members of the team are clear on the expectations of them in terms of authority, responsibility and accountability. _____

- The standard operating procedure for empowering people has been applied to every member of the team. _____

- Limits have been established to determine when the project plan will be revised, such as plus-or-minus 10-percent budget variation, etc. _____

- The needs of customers have been carefully considered in preparing the project plan. _____

- Qualitative guides have been developed for non-quantifiable project objectives, such as project performance (the "good" component of *good, fast, cheap*). ____

- Checklists have been prepared for major segments of the project so that nothing is overlooked. ____

Afterword

I welcome comments and suggestions on how the book could be improved in its next edition, and I would like to hear about your experiences in managing projects. You can write to me in care of my publisher or directly, using the following address:

James P. Lewis
302 Chestnut Mountain Drive
Vinton, VA 24179

Best of luck to each of you.

Notes

Chapter 1

1. See William Oncken, *Managing Management Time*. Englewood Cliffs, NJ: Prentice-Hall, 1984.

Chapter 2

1. Heal, David. "How to screw up." *Management Today*, September 1987, pp. 77–79.
2. Adapted from Rickards: see reading list.

Chapter 3

1. It is not necessary to develop a mission statement for a very small project. However, it is my opinion that all large projects should have a written mission statement.

2. PMI News, Vol. 2, No. 3, July 1987.

3. In projects, many objectives are ordered strictly by causal sequencing, and can be done using conventional network scheduling methods (see Chapter 5).

Chapter 4

1. The reader unfamiliar with statistics should consult a basic text, such as the one by Walpole, cited in the reading list, to see why this is true.

2. There must be a "Murphy's Law" involved here: everyone knows that *no* work activity ever takes less than the average time!

3. I understand that in some organizations game-playing is so firmly entrenched that a project manager cannot change it unilaterally. It is, nevertheless, not the way to run an organization.

4. Strictly speaking, this commentary belongs in the Control section of the book, but is placed here so that the subject of time cards can be covered in detail. Still, it is an important aspect of achieving good project control.

Chapter 5

1. For a detailed discussion of the history of scheduling methods, see Fleming, Bronn, and Humphries, in the reading list.

Chapter 7

1. Float will be used throughout this chapter as a generic term which could also apply to event slack.

2. I have used the term "man-days," rather than create a neutral term such as "person-days" to avoid awkward construction. Clearly, the term should be understood to include male or female workers.

Chapter 8

1. The reader who has no knowledge of statistics should consult a basic text before reading this chapter, since it is outside the scope of this work to explain the statistics involved. A suitable work is the book by Walpole, cited in the reading list.

2. I have paraphrased a passage from the book by Mendelssohn, *The Riddle of the Pyramids,* page 35. See reading list for complete citation.

3. Mendelssohn, page 35.

Chapter 9

1. See reading list for citation.

2. In some organizations, project managers do not deal with costs, but rather with *labor hours*. Once standard variance analysis has been presented in terms of cost, a method of dealing with working hours will be presented.

Chapter 10

1. See reading list for citation.

2. This is sometimes called the "Eichman defense." Eichman contended that he was only following orders, and that he was in no way responsible for the fate of the Jews in his concentration camp.

Chapter 12

1. See his book, *Thriving On Chaos* for more on this.

Chapter 13

1. See reading list.

2. Kouzes & Posner, pp. 7–8.

3. Kouzes & Posner have instruments available to measure how closely a leader conforms to the practices which they advocate. These can be ordered from University Associates, 8517 Production Ave., San Diego, CA, 92121.

4. See reading list.

5. Op. cit., p. 9.

6. McClelland, *Power, The Inner Experience*. See reading list.

7. R.L. Wing, *The Tao of Power*. Doubleday, 1986.

8. Rosenthal, R., & Jacobson, L. *Pygmalion in the Classroom*. New York: Holt, Rinehart, and Winston, 1968.

9. This description of the Rosenthal & Jacobson work has been simplified and stripped of its academic jargon, so that the person not familiar with the terminology can follow the essence of the results obtained. Those interested in a fuller exposition will find an excellent treatment in the book by Russel A. Jones, *Self-fulfilling Prophecies*, published by Lawrence Erlbaum Associates, 1977.

10. Instruments which measure a leader's conformance to the Hersey and Blanchard model can be ordered from University Associates, 8517 Production Ave., San Diego, CA 92121.

11. The word *behavior* is very important to note. This model deals only with how a leader behaves toward a follower, not with his or her attitude or feelings about the follower. Blake and Mouton have a model called the GRID™, which emphasizes the leader's attitude toward task and relationship, and is based on the self-fulfilling prophecy. The two models are very different, and should not be confused. See reading list for citation of Blake & Mouton's work.

12. Dr. Lawrence J. Peter, *The Peter Principle*.

Chapter 14

1. This was discussed in Chapter 13. It is reiterated here with an example which demonstrates that treating employees as though they are responsible does indeed accomplish that result.

Further Reading

Aaker, David A. *Developing Business Strategies*. New York: Wiley, 1984.

Adams, James L. *Conceptual Blockbusting: A Guide to Better Ideas*, second edition. New York: W.W. Norton, 1979.

Adams, John D. (Editor), *Transforming Leadership: From Vision to Results*. Alexandria, VA: Miles River Press, 1986.

Adams, John D. (Editor), *Transforming Work*. Alexandria, VA: Miles River Press, 1984.

Ailes, Roger. *You Are the Message: Secrets of the Master Communicators*. Homewood, IL: Dow Jones-Irwin, 1988.

Archibald, R. D., and Villoria, R.L., *Network-Based Management Systems (PERT/CPM)*. New York: Wiley, 1967.

Axelrod, Robert. *The Evolution of Cooperation*. New York: Basic Books, 1984.

Beer, Stafford. *Brain of the Firm*. Second Edition. Chichester, England: Wiley, 1981.

Beer, Stafford. *The Heart of Enterprise*. Chichester, England: Wiley, 1979.

Bennis, Warren G.; Benne, Kenneth D.; Chin, Robert; and Corey, Kenneth E. *The Planning of Change*. Third Edition. New York: Holt, Rinehart and Winston, 1976.

Bennis, Warren G., and Nanus, Burt. *Leaders: The Strategies for Taking Charge*. New York: Harper & Row, 1985.

Blake, Robert E., and Mouton, Jane S. *The Managerial Grid*. Houston, TX: Gulf Publishing, 1964.

Blanchard, Benjamin S. *Engineering Organization and Management*. Englewood Cliffs, NJ: Prentice-Hall, 1976.

Block, Peter. *The Empowered Manager*. San Francisco: Jossey-Bass, 1987.

de Bono, Edward. *New Think*. New York: Avon Books, 1971.

de Bono, Edward. *Six Thinking Hats*. Boston: Little, Brown & Co., 1985.

Burrill, Claude W., and Ellsworth, Leon W. *Modern Project Management*. Tenafly, NJ: Burrill-Ellsworth Assoc., 1980.

Calero, Henry H., and Oskam, Bob. *Negotiate the Deal You Want*. New York: Dodd, Mead & Company, 1983.

Cleland, David I., and King, William R. (Editors). *Project Management Handbook*. New York: Van Nostrand Reinhold, 1983.

Cleland, David I., and King, William R. *Systems Analysis and Project Management*. Second Edition. New York: McGraw-Hill, 1968, 1975.

Cohen, Herb. *You Can Negotiate Anything*. New York: Bantam, 1980.

Curtis, Dan B.; Mazza, J.M.; and Runnebohm, S. *Communication for Problem Solving*. New York: Wiley, 1979.

Davis, Philip J., and Park, David. *No Way: The Nature of the Impossible*. New York: W. H. Freeman, 1987.

Davis, Stanley M., and Lawrence, Paul R. *Matrix*. Reading, MA: Addison-Wesley, 1977.

Deal, T.E., and Kennedy, A.A. *Corporate Cultures: The Rites and Rituals of Corporate Life*. Reading, MA: Addison-Wesley, 1982.

Drucker, Peter F. *Innovation and Entrepreneurship*. New York: Harper & Row, 1985.

Drucker, Peter F. *Management: Tasks, Responsibilities, Practices*. New York: Harper & Row, 1974.

Dyer, William G. *Team Building: Issues and Alternatives*. Reading, MA: Addison-Wesley, 1977.

Fleming, Q.W.; Bronn, J. W.; and Humphreys, Gary C. *Project and Production Scheduling*. Chicago: Probus, 1987.

Fournies, Ferdinand F. *Coaching for Improved Work Performance*. New York: Van Nostrand, 1978.

Foster, Richard. *Innovation: The Attacker's Advantage*. New York: Summit Books, 1986.

Francis, Dave, and Young, Don. *Improving Work Groups: A Practical Manual for Team Building*. San Diego, CA: University Associates, 1979.

Hackman, J. Richard, and Oldham, Greg R. *Work Redesign*. Reading, MA: Addison-Wesley, 1980.

Harman, Willis, & Rheingold, Howard. *Higher Creativity: Liberating the Unconscious for Breakthrough Insights*. Los Angeles: Jeremy P. Tarcher, Inc., 1984.

Harvard Business Review of Management. New York: Harper & Row, 1975.

Harvard Business Review on Human Relations. New York: Harper & Row, 1979.

Harvey, Jerry B. *The Abilene Paradox: And Other Meditations on Management*. San Diego: University Associates, 1988.

Hersey, Paul. *The Situational Leader*. New York: Warner Books, 1984.

Hersey, Paul, and Blanchard, Kenneth. *Management of Organizational Behavior: Utilizing Human Resources*. Fourth Edition. Englewood Cliffs, NJ: Prentice-Hall, 1981.

Kanter, Rosabeth M. *The Change Masters*. New York: Simon & Schuster, 1984.

Kerzner, Harold. *Project Management: A Systems Approach to Planning, Scheduling, and Controlling*. New York: Van Nostrand, 1979.

Kouzes, James M., and Posner, Barry Z. *The Leadership Challenge: How to Get Extraordinary Things Done in Organizations*. San Francisco: Jossey-Bass, 1987.

Laborde, Genie Z. *Influencing with Integrity*. Palo Alto, CA: Syntony, 1984.

Lassey, W.R., and Sashkin, M. (Editors), *Leadership and Social Change*, Third Edition. San Diego: University Associates, 1983.

Lawler, E.E., III, *High-involvement Management*. San Francisco: Jossey-Bass, 1986.

Lax, David A., and Sebenius, James K. *The Manager as Negotiator*. New York: The Free Press, 1986.

Levitt, Theodore. *The Marketing Imagination*. New York: The Free Press, 1983.

Lynch, Dudley, and Kordis, Paul. *Strategy of the Dolphin: Scoring a Win in a Chaotic World*. New York: William Morrow & Company, 1988.

Maccoby, Michael. *Why Work: Leading the New Generation*. New York: Simon and Schuster, 1988.

Mali, Paul (Editor). *Management Handbook*. New York: Wiley, 1981.

Maciariello, Joseph A. *Program-Management Control Systems*. New York: Wiley, 1978.

March, James G., and Simon, Herbert A. *Organizations*. New York: Wiley, 1958.

McClelland, David. *Power: The Inner Experience*. New York: Irvington, 1975.

Mendelssohn, Kurt. *The Riddle of the Pyramids*. New York: Praeger, 1974.

Meredith, Jack R., and Mantel, Jr., Samuel J. *Project Management: A Managerial Approach*. New York: Wiley, 1985.

Miller, William C. *The Creative Edge: Fostering Innovation Where You Work*. Reading, MA: Addison-Wesley, 1986.

Mintzberg, Henry. *Mintzberg on Management: Inside Our Strange World of Organizations*. New York: The Free Press, 1989.

Moder, Joseph J.; Phillips, Cecil R.; and Davis, Edward W. *Project Management with CPM, PERT, and Precedence Diagramming*. Third Edition. New York: Van Nostrand, 1983.

Nierenberg, Gerard I. *The Complete Negotiator*. New York: Nierenberg & Zeif, 1986.

von Oech, Roger. *A Whack On the Side of the Head*. New York: Warner, 1983.

von Oech, Roger. *A Kick In the Seat of the Pants*. New York: Warner, 1986.

Oncken, Jr., William. *Managing Management Time*. Englewood Cliffs, NJ: Prentice-Hall, 1984.

Peters, Tom. *Thriving on Chaos*. New York: Alfred A. Knopf, 1987.

Pfeiffer, J. W.; Goodstein, L. D.; and Nolan, T. M. *Understanding Applied Strategic Planning: A Manager's Guide*. University Associates, 8517 Production Ave., San Diego, CA, 92121, 1985.

Project Management Journal. Project Management Institute, P.O. Box 43, Drexel Hill, PA 19026.

Ray, M., and Myers, R. *Creativity in Business*. Garden City, NY: Doubleday, 1986.

Reddy, W.B., and Jamison, K. (Editors). *Team Building: Blueprints for Productivity and Satisfaction*. Alexandria, VA: National Training Labs, 1988.

Rickards, Tudor. *Problem Solving Through Creative Analysis*. Epping, Essex, England: Gower Press, 1975.

Rifkin, Jeremy. *Time Wars*. New York: Touchstone, 1987.

Robert, Marc. *Managing Conflict From the Inside Out*. San Diego: University Associates, 1982.

Schumacher, E.F. *Small Is Beautiful: Economics As If People Mattered*. New York: Perennial Library, 1989 (reprint).

Slevin, Dennis P. *Executive Survival Manual: A Program for Managerial Effectiveness*. Pittsburgh, PA: Innodyne, P.O. Box 111386 (Zip 15238), 1985.

Walpole, Ronald E. *Introduction to Statistics*. Second Edition. New York: Macmillan, 1974.

Walton, Richard E. *Interpersonal Peacemaking: Confrontations and Third-Party Consultation*. Reading, MA: Addison-Wesley, 1969.

Waterman, Robert H. *The Renewal Factor*. New York: Bantam, 1987.

Watzlawick, P.; Beavin, J.; and Jackson, D. *Pragmatics of Human Communication*. New York: Norton, 1967.

Weisbord, Marvin R. *Productive Workplaces*. San Francisco: Jossey-Bass, 1987.

Winston, Stephanie. *The Organized Executive*. New York: Warner Books, 1983.

Index

About the
Author

James P. Lewis, Ph.D. is an experienced project manager, who now teaches seminars on the subject nationwide. His solid, no-nonsense approach is largely the result of the 15 years he spent in industry, working as an Electrical Engineer, engaged in the design and development of communication equipment. He held various positions, including Project Manager, Product Engineering Manager, and Chief Engineer, for Aerotron, Inc. and ITT Telecommunications, both of Raleigh, NC. He also was a Quality Manager for ITT Telecom, managing a department of 63 quality engineers, line inspectors, and test technicians.

While he was an engineering manager, he began working on a doctorate in organizational psychology, because of his conviction that a manager can only succeed by developing good interpersonal skills.

Altogether, Dr. Lewis has trained about 10,000 supervisors and managers in various aspects of management. He has written articles for *Training and Development Journal* and *Apparel Industry Magazine.* He has a B.S. in Electrical Engineering and a Ph. D. in Organizational Psychology, both from North Carolina State University in Raleigh. He is a member of several professional societies, including the American Psychological Association.

Jim is married to the former Lea Ann McDowell, and they live just outside Roanoke, Virginia, in the Blue Ridge Mountains. Although they have no biological children, they have four exchange student daughters, Yukiko Bono of Japan, Katarina Sigerud of Sweden, Susi Mraz of Austria, and Lin-Jeanette Larsen of Norway.

About the Publisher

PROBUS PUBLISHING COMPANY

Probus Publishing Company fills the informational needs of today's business professional by publishing authoritative, quality books on timely and relevant topics, including:

- Investing
- Futures/Options Trading
- Banking
- Finance
- Marketing and Sales
- Manufacturing and Project Management
- Personal Finance, Real Estate, Insurance and Estate Planning
- Entrepreneurship
- Management

Probus books are available at quantity discounts when purchased for business, educational or sales promotional use. For more information, please call the Director, Corporate/Institutional Sales at 1-800-PROBUS-1, or write:

Director, Corporate/Institutional Sales
Probus Publishing Company
1925 N. Clybourn Avenue
Chicago, Illinois 60614
FAX (312) 868-6250